JULY 2007
WORSHIP CONFERENCE

GOD SONGS

GOD SONGS

HOW TO WRITE AND SELECT SONGS FOR WORSHIP

PAUL BALOCHE
JIMMY & CAROL OWENS

GOD SONGS
How To Write And Select Songs For Worship

Baloche, Paul
   God songs : how to write and select songs for worship / Paul
   Baloche, Jimmy & Carol Owens. -- 1st ed. -- Lindale, Texas :
   Leadworship.com, 2004.

        p. ; cm.
        ISBN: 1-933150-03-3

        1. Church music–Writing and publishing. 2. Hymns–Writing and
   publishing. 3. Sacred songs–Writing and publishing.
   4. Composition (Music) I. Owens, Jimmy. II. Owens, Carol.
   III. Title.

BV335 .B35 2004
782.27/13–dc22   0412

All scripture quotations, unless otherwise indicated, are taken from the New
International Version®, copyright © 1973, 1978, 1984 by International Bible Society.
Used by permission of Zondervan Publishing House.

Scriptures designated NKJV are from the New King James Version
Copyright 1983 by Thomas Nelson, Inc.

ISBN 1-933150-03-3

Published by leadworship.com™
P.O. box 2101
Lindale, TX 75771
USA

Cover and interior design by Burnkit.

Printed in the United States of America

Attention Churches, Schools and Ministries: Copies of this book are available at
discounts for bulk purchases.

06 07 08 09 10 11 12 / 12 11 10 9 8 7 6 5

CONTENTS

PREFACE   11

INTRODUCTION   13
   Not Just for Songwriters   13
   What Attracts People to a Song?   15
   How to Use This Book   16

CHAPTER 1
HOW WORSHIP SONGS ARE BORN   23
   The Mystery of Music   23
   Capture the Moment   26
   Tuning In   26
   Life Set to Music   28
   Sing the Scriptures   29
   Sing Your Prayers   32
   Collecting and Organizing Your Thoughts 33
   Putting it all Together   33
   Writing on Assignment   34
   The Greenhouse   37
   From Inspiration to Perspiration   39

CHAPTER 2
WHAT MAKES A GREAT WORSHIP SONG?

The Cardinal Rule: All the elements working together to enhance the feeling of the message

The Very Idea! 44

The Right Title 46

The Building Blocks of a Song: Message Style Atmosphere Mood Form Lyrics Melody Harmony Rhythm

Hooks 48

Repetition Repetition Repetition 49

Hooks in Psalms 50

Beware the Blob 52

Common Song Forms 54

Unity in Variety 56

Other Song Forms 58

Tension and Release 58

Special Qualities of a Worship Song 60

Keeping it Simple 63

Songs for the Common Man 64

Easy to Learn 65

CHAPTER 3
WORDS THAT SING

The Sound of Words 71

Vowels and Consonants 71

Buzz Words 73

Two Words to Remember 74

Rhymes and Chimes 75

Rhyming Patterns 79

Conversing With God 80

Straight Ahead Lyrics 80

The Flow of Words 81

Sensory Lyrics—Images We Can See and Feel and Hear 82

Similes, Metaphors and Allegories 87

Strong Opening Lines 88

Just the Right Words 89

Solomon's Wisdom   89

A Short Course in Lyrical Photography: 90
  Snapshots Fresh Camera Angles Focus
  Lights ... Camera ... Action!

CHAPTER 4
MELODY THAT SOARS   97
  The Mystery of Melody   98
  Where Do Melodies Come From?   99
  The Influence of Scale Tones and Intervals   101
  The Ubiquitous 3rd   104
  Building Your Melody   105
  The Right Key   109
  The "Wings" of a Song   110
  The Staying Power of Great Melody   111

CHAPTER 5
HARMONY THAT ENHANCES   113
  The Mood-Enhancing Flavors and Colors of Harmony   114
  Tri—Tri Again   115
  Where Do Chords Come From?   115
  Inversions   118
  Why "Modern" Harmony?   120
  A Call to the Colors   120
  Get 'Em While They're Hot   121
  Chord Functions and Substitutions   126
  Non-Diatonic Chords   128
  Less is More   130
  What About Minor Harmony?   131
  Surprise!   131
  What to Leave Out?   133
  Changing Keys   133

CHAPTER 6
RHYTHM THAT MOVES (AND OTHER CONSIDERATIONS)   139
  Rhythm—the Groove and the Feel   139
  The Cardinal Rule in Arranging and Performance   142
  Intros, Figures, Fills and Endings   143
  Think Syncopation   144

RHYTHMIC AND DYNAMIC VARIETY 148

REHEARSE REHEARSE REHEARSE 150

THE IMPORTANCE OF STYLE 150

KNOW THE STYLES 151

CHAPTER 7
WORDS AND MUSIC, HAPPY TOGETHER 155

MATCHING WORDS TO MELODIES 155

UPS AND DOWNS—THE IMAGERY OF LINES 159

APPROPRIATENESS 160

SETTING SCRIPTURE TO MUSIC 161

TRANSLATING 165

CHAPTER 8
HOW TO STIMULATE CREATIVITY 167

TWELVE KEYS TO UNLOCK WRITER'S BLOCK 167

TWELVE TOOLS TO MAKE YOUR JOB EASIER 172

LET'S GET TOGETHER AND WRITE A SONG 174

FREE-FOR-ALL SONGWRITING? 179

BUILDING YOUR CRAFT— 180

FOUR DISCIPLINES OF A SONGWRITER: LISTEN ANALYZE WRITE REWRITE

RECAP: SIXTEEN QUALITIES OF A WORSHIP SONG 183

HOW DO I KNOW WHEN MY SONG IS REALLY READY? .. 184

CHAPTER 9
GETTING YOUR SONGS HEARD 187

BREAKING AND ENTERING 188

ATTITUDE CHECK 194

DON'T QUIT YOUR DAY JOB 195

BE THE BEST YOU CAN BE 195

WHAT'S YOUR CALLING? 196

MAKING DEMOS 198

PLACING YOUR SONGS 199

CCLI 203

CHAPTER 10

MUSIC THAT MINISTERS

THREE MINISTRIES 207

ANOINTING OIL 209

SELECTING SONGS FOR A SPECIFIC OCCASION 212

HYMNS OR CHORUSES? 215

NEW LIFE FOR OLD HYMNS 218

TIMELINESS OR TIMELESSNESS 219

WORSHIP FOR KIDS 220

EXTRA TECHNIQUES TO CONSIDER—LINING; CALL AND RESPONSE 224

CODA: GO FOR IT!

SCRIPTURAL ROOTS 227

THE ORIGINS OF CONTEMPORARY CHRISTIAN MUSIC 229

LEARNING FROM THE PAST 231

POP MUSIC IN THE BIBLE? 231

DIFFERENT STROKES 232

WATCH FOR NEW DIRECTIONS 233

THE WAY OF THE VISIONARY 234

THE LONE RANGER BITES THE DUST 237

BE A VOICE FOR GOD 238

A NEW DAY 242

A WORLDWIDE PHENOMENON 244

THE AWESOME POWER OF MUSIC 244

THE EXPLOSIVE POTENTIAL 248

GO FOR IT! 249

CHECKLIST FOR SONGWRITERS (OR SELECTORS) 253

APPENDIX 1 SONG TYPES THAT HAVE NOT MADE IT

257

APPENDIX 2 THE ABC'S OF MUSIC

261

GLOSSARY

277

ABOUT THE AUTHORS

281

SCRIPTURES RELATED TO WORSHIP

289

INDEX

300

PREFACE

*My heart is stirred by a noble theme as I recite my verses
for the King; my tongue is the pen of a ready writer.*

Psa 45:1 (NIV)

I can feel this God song rising up in me.

From *Hallelujah! (Your Love is Amazing)* by
Brenton Brown and Brian Doerksen

What are God Songs? God Songs are songs sung to God, for God and about God. We sing because God sings, and we are made in His image. God sings? Yes! Zephaniah 3:17(NKJV) says, "The Lord your God in your midst, the Mighty One, will save...He will rejoice over you with singing." That's the ultimate God song! God singing over us. If we could hear such a song we would fall down in awe.

There's another kind of God song that requires neither talent nor craft. It might be a momentary cry—a new song sung to the Lord from a thrilled or saddened heart. It may be the simplest child-like expression of love and faith, a song unique to the worshiper, a momentary "singing in the spirit," which no one else will ever sing. That's a God song too. The Father hears it and is blessed, not because of its dazzling craftsmanship, but because of the love and trust it expresses, even as a dad takes delight in the smeared valentine offered by his little child, who made it just for him.

But in this book we're talking about writing (or selecting) songs for the church to sing together, songs of worship that express, in words we all can share in, our love for Him. That kind of song does require talent—a songwriting gift, developed by its recipient to a higher level.

These God Songs begin with the exciting spark of inspiration that is born out of our own worship. Then they are molded in the crucible of our craft. Powerful, singable God Songs adore, praise and witness; but more, they are special because they are not only glorious truths, but good songs. What the Spirit ignites in our spirits is forged and formed into art in the furnace of hard work and dedication to excellence. Great God Songs have both fresh, original expressions of truth, and the musical integrity that make them easy to remember and hard to forget. Great God Songs are the songs that hit us right in the heart.

INTRODUCTION

God Songs is a cross between a textbook, a reference book and a conversation with three songwriters. Our purpose is simple; it's to help up-and-coming writers produce good worship songs—moving, memorable—songs that help usher people into an awareness of God's presence. Whether you're a beginner or a pro, this book can help you.

A wise man once said, "There are three rules for writing the perfect song. Unfortunately, no one seems to remember what they are." Actually, Rule One is that there are no rules. But there are *principles.* There are observable, definable *qualities* common to effective songs of all kinds.

Song styles come and go, but, sacred or secular, in any genre or generation, the underlying *principles* that make a song work (or not work) remain the same. We won't bind you up with a set of *rules;* we'll simply point out those principles, and hope to stimulate you in a wonderful experience of discovery that will become an ongoing part of your life.

Not Just for Songwriters

If you're a worship leader (or lead worshiper, as some prefer) but not (yet?) a songwriter, this book is for you, too. **The principles you need to**

understand in *writing* worship songs are the same ones you need to understand in *choosing* them. Your knowledge of the qualities that make songs spiritually powerful, easy to learn, easy to sing and hard to forget, will determine whether or not your people enter into worship easily and without distraction.

So whether you write or program praise and worship songs, contemporary Christian music, or wholesome entertainment, this book will help you find your full potential. But our main emphasis will be on those *specific* characteristics that make worship songs more effective.

In the book you'll find personal experiences from many of your favorite songwriters, telling you how their songs were born. You'll get good advice from a prominent worship music publisher as well.

So, (with a little help from our friends) we'll help you discover the secrets of successful songs. Many of these are open secrets—hidden in plain sight and available to anyone who knows what to look for. *God Songs* will help you recognize them and make them an instinctive part of your own writing or song selection process.

And who knows? Maybe you're a latent songwriter who hasn't discovered it yet. After reading this book, you may decide, "I can do that!" and start writing songs of your own.

Defining Our Scope

Let's define the scope of this book. Although it has devotional and motivational portions, it's mainly a *how-to* book on writing and choosing songs for worship, as the subtitle says. There are good books on the theology of worship and the lifestyle of a worshiper, and we recommend them. Don't let the fact that we aren't constantly preaching, teaching and urging motivational values make you think we don't care about them. We do. They are foundational. A worship leader should lead a life of worship, and so should a writer of songs for worship. Songs should be scriptural and anointed by the Holy Spirit in order to accomplish their purpose. But in this book we start with the assumption that this foundation has already been laid; that you, our reader, are a born-again Christian, a worshiper, dedicated to serving the Lord with the spiritual and musical gifts entrusted to you, and we want to help you improve those gifts. (By the way, when you add -er or -ed or -ing to *worship*, how many p's does it get? According to the dictionaries, one is preferred, but two is correct also.)

What Attracts People to a Song?

Most people don't know what attracts them to a song; they only know whether or not they like it. But you, as a songwriter or lead worshiper, have a great advantage if you understand those definable, reproducible qualities that touch people in ways that make them want to hear a song over and over again.

Wouldn't it be wonderful if every time you wrote a song you could run it by a panel of the world's great songwriters to critique it and help you make it the best it can be? Most of us don't have access to that kind of help. But we hope to provide you with a helpful tool—a way to critique your own songs by professional standards. At the back of the book you'll find a Songwriter's (or Selector's) Checklist, consisting of 30 qualities common to great songs of all kinds. We hope you'll use it as a reference resource for the rest of your songwriting life: a measuring rod to critique and improve your own songs. It isn't a magic formula, but the more of these qualities your song has going for it, the more likely it is to reach its potential.

How to Use This Book

- We suggest you go through the book at least twice. First read the whole thing. The second time through, just pick out the headings and the words in bold print. The headings (same as the Table of Contents) are an outline, and the bolded words in the text are key thoughts, to jog your memory once you've read the book through.

- To make your experience with the book even more practical, select one or more of your songs, preferably unpublished, and use them as work pieces as you go through the book, checking them against one principle after another. Keep a copy of your original versions. (Never erase anything! You may decide you did it right the first time around.) Compare your finished work with your original and see how you've improved it.

- After that, use the book as a reference, especially the *Application* sections and the *Songwriter's Checklist*, to refresh your memory, to strengthen your songs, and always to keep improving.

- A song manufactured from a formula may be correct, but may lack warmth, spontaneity and emotion. So the idea is not to write *from* the checklist (although that may help a writer in the learning stages) but to absorb the principles into your own writing process, let your song flow, then check it against the list to see if you can eliminate its weaknesses and strengthen its strengths. Your ingrained knowledge of techniques will help you hone, polish and distill your song until it's the best you can make it before you offer it to the public.

Authors' note:

Three authors: Who's saying what? Most of the time you won't know, and it doesn't matter. Although we each may have different specialties, we've known each other for a long time and teach a lot of the same things. We teach by the tag team method: any one of us can jump in. But there are certain places where one of us will do an analysis of another's lyrics while the lyricist looks embarrassed and says, "Aw, shucks. Thanks, guys."(If we're analyzing our own stuff we may not tell you.) The devotional passages are by Carol.

As we were finishing this book, we submitted a draft to a number of leaders for criticism. Some asked us to go back and insert some stories of our personal history as songwriters. So, we did. The few we've included are not for personal boasting, but to encourage you to see new possibilities and a broader vision for your music. One day you may write a special little tune, send it out there with your others, and lo and behold, it will be the start of something extraordinary. The Lord will breathe on it, and away it will go, accomplishing things you've never even thought about. Think, for example, of how Les Garrett must have felt when he turned on the TV news to hear "This is the Day" being sung in German by the crowd tearing down the Berlin wall!

Like many other writers whose work has had some unusual impact, we can tell you that we didn't try to break down doors and make these things happen. Often we were little more than spectators, watching God use the best we had to offer, and astounded at the results.

Paul

I was playing guitar at my church in New Jersey and just beginning to lead worship now and then, when my wife Rita and I felt a call to go down to Lindale, Texas to work with the ministry of Keith and Melody Green. Keith was gone by then, but Melody and several volunteers were carrying on the mission of Last Days Ministries. There we met Jimmy and Carol Owens for the first time. Being a fairly new Christian, I was unaware of their background in pioneering so much of what is now referred to as "Contemporary Christian Music." Everyone else knew who they were and it seemed like everyone had a story of how their lives were impacted by this dynamic couple. The first year we were there, Melody hosted an "Artist Retreat" for Christian musicians. Artists like Steven Curtis Chapman, Dallas Holm, The Second Chapter of Acts and many others attended these powerful days of prayer and refreshing.

During one of the prayer times Jimmy and Carol shared how they felt like God was telling them to "go to seed"— to begin laying down their own musical vision and become seed for the ministry of others. "Unless a seed is planted in the ground and dies, it abides alone" was one of the scriptures that they felt were speaking to them. As a result of this new direction they started School of Music Ministries International, or SMMI.

The vision was to raise up and equip worshipers around the world to become more skilled in leading others in worship and impacting their culture for Christ. It was a month long school held several times a year in the U.S. and overseas. They asked me to play and teach guitar in the school and lead the bands for various guest worship leaders such as Marty Nystrom, Bob Fitts, Dan and Jamie (Owens)Collins.

Jimmy and Carol were, and still are, the kind of people who see things in other people's lives and help bring them out. Looking back, I'm so grateful for their willingness to entrust me with being part of those early schools. It helped shape and define the course of my ministry over the years with an emphasis on discipling others in worship ministry. From Southeast Asia to

Texas to Africa to England to Eastern Europe to Australia, they and their teams raised up schools of worship before most of the "worship conferences" we've grown accustomed to existed.

In fact, I remember Maranatha! Music modeling their first "worship workshops" after Jimmy and Carol's original vision. I believe much of the explosion in worship that we are witnessing today can be partly attributed to their investment in the lives of leaders around the world in the early nineties. They even invited a little known Australian to teach vocal-group singing in one of their early schools. The backup singer's name was Darlene Zschech, and she was just beginning to lead worship at Hillsong Church in Sydney. She's now one of the best known worship leaders and writers of worship songs in the world. Jimmy and Carol have always cared greatly to see people raised up with the "right heart" as well as the right skills necessary to carry out that heart. They live it, model it, and teach it. They have devoted their lives to music ministry and songs. They have the "fruit on the tree."

I invite you as Jimmy, Carol and I put our heads together, tell our stories, and share insights that we hope will inspire your own writing to bear good fruit.

Paul's Acknowledgments:

I would like to thank my amazing wife, Rita–I love living the journey with you. You have been my greatest mentor and inspiration for writing songs. And to Sarah, David, and Cherie– Being your Dad is my greatest joy.

I'm grateful to all the people who inspired or nurtured in me the desire to write songs that the church can sing back to God: Rita Baloche, Dan Willard, Kelly Willard, Lenny LeBlanc, Pastor Albie Pearson, Pastor Tracy Hanson, Ed Kerr, Claire Cloninger, John Chisum, Jimmy & Carol Owens, Don Harris, Marty Nystrom, Craig Dunnagan, believers and friends from Community Christian Fellowship as well as many, many faithful worship leaders and songwriters around the world who have challenged and inspired me to dig down deep as I reach up to God with songs of worship.

Special thanks to Frank DeJong for your friendship and tireless effort in finishing this book.

Jimmy, Carol, and Paul would like to thank Curt Coffield, Pete Episcopo, Sean Swanson, Tom Kraeuter, Glenn Hegel, Dan Perrin, and Shane Meyer for reading our early manuscript and giving us some valuable feedback.

Jimmy and Carol's Acknowledgments:

(At the risk of slapping our foreheads and saying, "Who did we leave out?")

In our journey, thanks to the friends who were there for us at the turning points: Pastor Earl Sexauer, who fathered us in the ministry; Pastor Jake Bellig, who let us experiment in making church music contemporary; Audrey Meier, who got us our first recording opportunity; Ralph Carmichael, who launched us as songwriter/artists; Albie and Helen Pearson, who helped us through the hard spots; Al Kasha, who taught us to write better songs and showed us the heart of a teacher; Christian Artists, who gave us platforms to teach in the U.S. and Europe; Pastor Jack Hayford, who equipped us and sent us out; Jean and Elmer Darnall, who ushered us into international ministry; Pat Boone, Buck and Annie Herring, the Second Chapter of Acts, Barry McGuire, Wendell Burton, Andrae Crouch, Tramaine Hawkins, The Imperials, Michael and Stormie Omartian, Dean Jones and so many others, whose performances made our music come to life; David and Dale Garratt, pioneers in modern worship; Loren Cunningham, who gave us the vision for School of Music Ministries International; Joseph Sim, Isaac Lim, Kang Ho Soon and Tay Wei Lien, who opened up Singapore and Southeast Asia to us; Melody Green, who provided an American home for SMMI; Rich and Pam Boyer, who always had a place for us; Buddy Owens, for enthusiastically touring, singing, and roady-ing in the early years, and for serious editing help later; Dan and Jamie (Owens) Collins, who have traveled, taught, sung, produced and been a part of our ministry in every possible way. And to all who have ever taught and toured with us, our deepest thanks. Thanks be to God... for everything!

CHAPTER 1
HOW WORSHIP SONGS ARE BORN

Worship is not music, but music can be worship. God must love music, because the Bible says there's a lot of it in heaven and invites us to come before His presence with singing (Psalm 100:2.) If we use music as an expression of our love to the Lord, He is pleased, and we're refreshed. God made us that way.

Music feeds the soul as food feeds the body. Combining the power of the Word, the Holy Spirit and music is like a three-fold cord that is not easily broken. That's why the worship movement today is so explosive; it feeds both spirit and soul. It fills a longing many of us didn't even realize we had.

The Mystery of Music

To most people music is a mysterious thing and so are musicians. If you're serious about your ministry as a musician, serious to the point that you sometimes space out or forget to eat, you've probably discovered that your friends and folks worry about you. They don't understand exactly what it is you *do*. **As a Christian songwriter, especially a worship songwriter,**

what you do is lead people in expressing their love and worship to the Lord—honoring, adoring and venerating Him. You have the holy privilege of putting words into the mouths of God's people—wonderful words that they might not have thought of saying to the Lord before. Or perhaps saying ancient words in a new way. It's a precious privilege, to be valued and taken seriously. A songwriter can be a soul doctor, a healer. We're handling nuclear, life-impacting material. So let's handle it with awe, with reverence, with care, with thankfulness, with humility, and with joy.

As we write, let's hope among other things that our songs will:

Magnify the worth of God and bring Him pleasure.

Teach the doctrinal truths of scripture.

Evoke a whole-hearted response to the revelation of God's love and character.

Inspire others to live their lives for the glory of God.

Motivate others to know Him and enjoy Him.

Help others become more aware of His presence in their lives.

If we're going to suggest that the church, with its rich heritage of great music, should use our songs in its holy mission, we had better make sure ours are as empowered as those we would have them replace.

Lord make us a holy people
Turn our hearts to righteousness again
Take away our sin
Fill our thirsty souls again

Visit us with the Holy Spirit
In the beauty of holiness descend
Like a mighty wind
Fill our thirsty souls again

Come like fire
Or come like the gentle rain
But fill our thirsty souls again

As we wait in the stillness
Come, Holy Spirit
Oh come
And fill our thirsty souls again
Fill our thirsty souls again

(Fill Our Thirsty Souls Again, from *Heal Our Land*, by Jimmy and Carol Owens)

Shop Talk

Before we move on, let's define a couple of terms we'll be using throughout the book:

1. What do we mean by a *worship* song? A song doesn't have to be congregational to be a worship song, but for the purposes of this discussion, we're defining a worship song as a song to be sung together by a group of worshipers, or congregation.

2. In worship music lingo, a worship song is often referred to as a *chorus*, regardless of how many sections it has. But since *chorus* can also mean a repeated section of a song, we'll try to use the term *chorus* only for that. We'll call a "worship chorus" a *worship song*. In conversation you'll probably continue to use the terms interchangeably.

Capture the Moment

Many of the most prolific worship song writers are worship leaders. But **you don't *have* to be a lead worshiper to write good worship songs, you just need to be a worshiper.** The best worship songs usually are not crafted for commercial purposes. Some of them, or at least the beginning "nuggets," come when you're not even trying to write a song.

Darlene Zschech put it so well when someone asked what sparks a song in her. She said you read, or hear, or see something that causes passion and you go, "Hey!" That says it, Darlene. You go, "Hey!" You're looking for that. "Hey!"—that spark—that something, that gives birth to an idea that ignites the process of writing a song. The strength of that "Hey!" may well determine the strength of the song.

Many of the best are born in church. The presence of the Holy Spirit is like oil, lubricating our spirits, causing music to flow. Maybe something in the worship— a word, a phrase, a line—sparks off something in you, and you continue singing your own worship phrases in your heart, spinning off into your own melody. When that happens, write it down! Write it down! Write it down! No, you won't remember it, so use the back of the bulletin or your PDA or the trusty notepad that you *always* carry for such occasions. Later, you can take your inspired idea out and worship with it until more of it falls into place.

Or sometimes the sermon sparks an idea. You think, 'We need a song that says that. Even the title would make a good hook!' It's rare that you get more than about 15% of a song that way, but you may have enough for a great start. Thank the Lord for the nugget, save it and put it away for later.

Tuning In

Always have your antennae up. A large part of a songwriter's job is to find and retrieve inspiration. Notice the way words are put together, how they sound, how they will sing. Capture little phrases that will become hooks. You hear a good one and say to yourself, "Hey, that could make a good song." Then be a doodler; remember, write it down. Get the *heart*, the human *emotion* from the nugget; that's what makes the song work.

Listen to what the people of God are saying when they pray or praise. It shows you what they need and how they feel. Try to incorporate these into your songs. Go ahead and open your eyes and jot down what somebody is praying. If you feel odd about doing that, be at peace. Somebody wrote down what Moses prayed and Hannah prophesied.

During some of our workshops Jimmy went through a stage when he felt he was getting too analytical, writing notes during worship times. He was concerned that he was missing out on the feeling of worship. But the Lord helped him to see that that was his calling, to study and be able to teach others, and that while he might miss out on some of the *feelings* of worship because of the busyness of his mind, what he was doing was an act of worship in itself.

HOW THE SONG WAS BORN
Paul: Revival Fire Fall

Paul was at a Youth With A Mission meeting when people were shouting out prayers: "Pour out your Spirit, Lord!" "We lift up your name!" "Send your fire, Lord!" "Send revival!" "Fall on us, Holy Spirit!" And he heard in his mind the phrase, *Revival fire fall!* "Hey, that feels good in the mouth. It will sing great and it says something vital." Paul wrote that song during the service and taught it to the people at the end. It capsulized what they had been praying. It became a theme song each night at the Brownsville Revival and spread from there all over the world.

You're writing for the moment. Capture a *moment* that gives you a subject and an emotion. Pull down something from Jesus. If nothing else it's a good spiritual exercise.

Find that nugget, pull it down. It's like a little gift from heaven. It's all from God, and it all goes back to God.

Life Set to Music

Songwriting is a way of journaling your journey. King David wrote out of his life experiences, even his bad ones: when he fled from Absolom, his son (Psalm 3); when the Lord delivered him from the hand of Saul (Psalm 18); when he pretended to be insane before Abimelech (Psalm 34); when Nathan the prophet came to him after he had sinned with Bathsheba (Psalm 51). (Also, check out Psalms 7, 30, 56, 57, 142)

HOW THE SONG WAS BORN
Bart Millard: "I Can Only Imagine"

When Bart was 19 years old, his father died. He heard all the cliches about how wonderful Heaven was, but somehow he couldn't get a grip on it. As he struggled with eternity, he found himself writing the phrase "I can only imagine" over and over again. He says, "I did know Dad was in a better place, and that started me thinking about what he was seeing there; things we could never fathom here. It brought peace and hope to me..." Years later, he rediscovered that phrase in a journal. "So, I decided to enlarge on what had been in my heart for so long. It was one of those 'God things' where it was literally written in five minutes—but it was something that had been on my heart for ten years." The song was written by a grieving son crying out to God for answers. Now his song is helping others heal. The song, born out of sorrow, reached number one on radio airplay charts and won three Dove awards.

Sing the Scriptures

Often your songs may spring out of the Word of God as you meditate on it in your quiet times. A passage touches something deep in you and begins to set itself to music. Here's a good exercise to try. Shut yourself in a quiet place where no one can hear you. It's very important that you not feel self conscious. If you don't have a place of solitude, just find the most private place you can and sing under your breath, or at whatever level you feel comfortable.

Open your Bible to a psalm and begin to sing it aloud, improvising in real time. Read slightly ahead, making up the melody as you go. Maybe it's a psalm where the psalmist pours out his heart to the Lord. *Feel* all the emotions and express them spontaneously with the words. At times you'll find yourself singing ringing high tones on words of high praise, at other times almost whispering anguished cries of the psalmist's heart, possibly in minor modes.

What this sounds like will differ from person to person, depending on one's musical background. It probably won't have any form but will be more like "stream of consciousness," or like a recitative from an opera or oratorio. Don't worry about that—it's because there is probably no metrical form in the passage you're singing. If you're a good improvising instrumentalist, you may want to accompany yourself with appropriate chords. Even if you tape this for your own amazement, don't consider it a song. No one else is likely to sing it. It's very private. You may however, as a byproduct, come up with a line or two worth developing into a real song. Whether or not you do, you will be practicing valuable lessons of setting emotions to music.

HOW THE SONG WAS BORN

Darlene Zschech: Shout to the Lord

"'Shout to the Lord' came while I was having a quiet time with the Lord," Darlene says. "It was one of those dark days in my life, and I turned to the Lord for peace." She sat at the piano, opened her Bible to the Psalms and started singing. The song took form and she sang it over and over again and it lifted her spirit.

Darlene ventured to sing the song for her worship pastor and another team member at Hills Church, where she sang in the worship team. "I could hardly play it, I was so nervous. I kept starting and stopping and apologizing." Finally she made them stand with their backs to her as she sang to them. When they praised the song enthusiastically, she thought they were just being nice.

The worship team sang the song in church, and before it was even recorded, Darlene was amazed to start getting letters from all over the world from people who were singing it in their churches.

What started as the cry of a worshiper's heart has resonated with the hearts of believers all over the world.

HOW THE SONG WAS BORN

Rick Founds: Lord, I Lift Your Name on High

The cross is the central doctrine of the New Testament. Why are there so few modern worship songs that include something so vital? Rick, the worship leader for a large church, targeted that need with "Lord, I Lift Your Name On High" and gave us the most awesome thing in the world to sing about. It came out of his personal devotions as he accompanied his scripture reading with his guitar. How's that for unique? As he contemplated the earth's cycle of clouds and rain, the scriptures showed him the cycle of Jesus coming from heaven, going to the cross for us, rising from the dead and returning home again. He says, "The response to grasping even a little of that is praise, thanksgiving and gratitude." He has heard his song done in every style you can think of. "It's a lot of fun to hear things you've written done in reggae, in 3/4, in country, and in Spanish flavor. That means those groups have made the song their own. It's exciting!"

HOW THE SONG WAS BORN

Rita Baloche: Rock of Ages

Rita says, "I always wanted to write a song with a rock beat about God my Rock. I wanted to boldly proclaim God's greatness with a bold music medium. As I read in 1 Samuel 2:2, Hannah had the words that inspired these two ideas to come together in this song: 'There is no Rock like our God!'"

Sing Your Prayers

If you're one of those who are immersed in music and find yourself singing much of the time, try singing your prayers to the Lord, as well. King David did. A good time to do this is when you're driving in your car, alone. You'll find your music taking on the feeling of the burdens or praises of your heart. It can intensify your prayer life. Caution: Do not attempt to accompany yourself on your guitar while driving.

Paul:

If I could give you one line about writing worship songs, it would be 'Sing your prayers.' This is because most of our prayers tend to come from a sincere, authentic place in our heart, the very kinds of expressions we're trying to write in our songs.

HOW THE SONG WAS BORN

Matt Redman: The Heart of Worship

When Matt's home church was trying to find a "missing dynamic" in their worship, the pastor "dismissed the band and sound system for a season, and we gathered together with just our voices. His point was that we'd lost our way in worship, and the way to get back to its heart would be to strip everything away." It worked. Eventually, people met God in a new way, singing a cappella and praying aloud.

From this, the lyrics came: "When the music fades, all is stripped away, and I simply come, Longing just to bring back something that's of worth that will bless your heart ... I'm coming back to the heart of worship, and it's all about You, Jesus."

When the church reintroduced the band, they had gained a new perspective. "Worship is all about Jesus, and He commands a response in the depths of our souls no matter what the circumstance and setting. 'The Heart of Worship' simply describes what occurred."

Collecting and Organizing Your Thoughts

Once you've decided what you're writing about, you'll need a way to organize your thoughts—to pull together everything you know about this subject. An excellent way to do this is called **"clustering,"** which works for prose, poetry, lyrics—any kind of writing.

- First write down your topic in the center of a page.

- Then *cluster* around it all the ideas, key words, phrases, and images that occur to you on that subject. Ideas will spring off ideas. Don't try to force them, just let them flow spontaneously from the right, or creative, side of your brain, in whatever order they come.

- Don't try to organize them yet, and don't be too critical of ideas that may at first seem far-fetched. Just keep writing down whatever occurs until the flow stops and the subject seems exhausted.

- Now put the left, or organizational, side of your brain to work: outlining, sequencing, structuring, eliminating unnecessary or peripheral aspects, and honing in on the essence of your message. You may find that much of your lyric writes itself or falls into place more easily using this method.

Pulling it all Together

When you're writing, you can start just about anywhere: the melody, the lyric, the melody and lyric together, the chord progression. Go with whatever comes to mind first. Sometimes a song behaves itself properly and starts itself at the beginning, progressing logically through to the end like a well-told story. Sometimes it doesn't. If the hook line for the chorus presents itself first, which is often the case, write it down and go from there, working backward and forward as the ideas come. Any way that works is the right way.

The ideal process of writing a Christian song should be not only a co-operation of the left and right sides of the brain, but a collaboration of the writer's spirit with the Holy Spirit, producing an anointed and appointed message instigated by God and crafted by the writer.

Writing on Assignment

Not every song begins with an inspiration. Some are born out of a need. Your pastor needs a song to go with a particular message he's going to preach, and you can't find one. A publisher or an artist needs a song on a certain subject to fill a spot. Or a program needs a theme song. Professional songwriters are often called on to write to order. This is where craftsmanship comes in. First, gather all the pertinent facts that need to go into the message, cluster them, pray and commit your way to the Lord, and let your God-given creativity take over. **Even though the song didn't start from an emotional experience, it can still be anointed.**

HOW THE SONG WAS BORN

Rita Baloche: I Will Celebrate

Rita saw a need and filled it. She says, "Our youth went to a Christian concert to hear Mylon LeFevre. His message of God's salvation was clear and his music was alive. The kids really responded to it. I wished the music at church could be as lively and accessible to draw in the young and young at heart. Driving home that night, I sang this "new song" to myself. When I arrived at the house I played the idea on the piano for my husband, Paul. Paul played it for me the second time through, and though I've sung it many times, I never played it again. I married a great accompanist!"

Paul:

Integrity Music used to put out a newsletter to a group of songwriters to make them aware of certain worship recordings that needed new songs. Sometimes they would furnish themes or scriptures that pointed the writers in a certain direction. 'Sing Out!' was a song written for Ron Kenoly. Ron requested songs from writers about building the temple of God from the first chapters of II Chronicles. So, Ed Kerr and I spent some time in that area of scripture and began to mull over II Chronicles 1-5, writing down key phrases, certain words like "a palace of praise," "a throne of thanksgiving," "building a temple here for the Lord." And just that phrase "Sing Out!" felt like a good working title. It was one of those that we actually worked on for a whole week, lyrically and musically, until it felt strong. It ended up being the title of Ron's project *Sing Out!*

Some songs come quickly. Others take a long time. Bob Fitts wrote "Blessed Be the Lord God Almighty" in five or ten minutes. Tim Hughes gestated "Here I Am to Worship" for nine months before it was born. Chris Tomlin's "Forever" seemed to take forever—he worked on it off and on for four years.

35

||||||||||||||||||||||||||||||||||||||||||||||||||||||||||||||||||||||||||||||||||||||||||||||||||||||||||||||||||||||||||||||||||||||||||||||||

HOW THE SONG WAS BORN
Chris Tomlin: Forever

Chris says, "The gift God has given me is to write things that are simple and connect with people quickly." Sometimes, writing *simply* takes a lot of skill, and a lot of time. Chris spent four years on "Forever." The verses came quickly, but the chorus just wouldn't work right. He says, "I hoped someone else would come up with a chorus. Then one day in a recording studio, I was sitting there singing, 'Forever God is faithful, forever God is …' and I couldn't come up with the next word. Then our bass player's wife, Janet, stuck her head in the door and said, 'strong.' Just like that, it clicked."And it clicked with the church, too. Chris says, "It still blows me away that people know it so well."

||||||||||||||||||||||||||||||||||||||||||||||||||||||||||||||||||||||||||||||||||||||||||||||||||||||||||||||||||||||||||||||||||||||||||||||||

HOW THE SONG WAS BORN
Tim Hughes: Here I Am To Worship

Tim says, "I was playing around with my guitar when the verse just came out." But the chorus eluded him. Nine months passed before he patched it together with another strong melody idea and had the entire song. The lyrical theme came to him from the scriptures.

"I'd been thinking through Jesus' amazing sacrifice," he says."Sometimes when God meets us, we don't know how to respond properly. It's often too much for us to take in. Hopefully, in a small way, the chorus captures that: 'Here I am to worship. Here I am to bow down. Here I am to say that you're my God. Altogether lovely, worthy, wonderful.'

"The main motivation behind the song was to capture a response to Jesus giving up his throne in heaven, ultimately to die on a cross. It has been a real privilege to see how God has used the song."

Brian Doerksen: Come, Now Is the Time to Worship

Brian Doerksen says, "For me this song is a 'life message' song, even though I wrote it in a few days. I feel like it took years of leading worship and the heartbreaks and joys of life to get to the place of being ready to write it." He says, "I wrote it as a call to worship incorporating key things I believe about worship." He believes God wants us to come to Him just as we are, though "when true worship happens, we don't stay the way we are. When we make that choice, we experience the pleasure of worship: the treasure of being with God." That's where those wonderful lines come from: "One day every tongue will confess You are God, One day every knee will bow/ Still the greatest treasure remains for those who gladly choose You now."

The Greenhouse

Paul likes to compare the writing process this way: **Creating a song is a lot like having a little plant growing in your greenhouse**. It's good to have lots of little plants at various stages growing there. Not all of your ideas turn out to be worth pursuing, but some of them may grow into beautiful flowers. Don't try to hurry it, or force it to grow, just visit it occasionally, worship a little with it, and see if anything more comes. Spirit-birthed songwriting is an organic process. Our songs grow out of the seed of God's word that's planted in us, nurtured by the warmth of our fellowship with Him. As our relationship grows, our understanding and our conversations (songs) with Him deepen. God reveals Himself to us in new ways and we want to sing those thoughts back to Him as we understand Him more.

Don't take a song out of the greenhouse too soon. (Remember the old TV ad slogan, "We will sell no wine before its time.") Eventually you'll need to apply your knowledge of the craft to it and finish up the song, but don't be in too big a hurry to get into the edit mode, unless you've gotten yourself into a deadline situation.

Try to avoid arbitrary deadlines. They just put unnecessary pressure on you and cause you to release songs before they're really ready. There are lots of 70% songs out there. If the writers had just waited a little longer before considering them finished, perhaps they would have ended up with a 100% song.

"Deadlines are a two-edged sword," Paul says. "Sometimes they can light a fire under you and put a sense of urgency in your writing. But there are several songs that I feel could have been stronger if I had had a little more time to brood over them. Many of the songs made the recording deadline but I can't help thinking in hindsight how much stronger they could have been if given more time."

See what grows by itself for a while. **There will probably come a moment when you realize that that's about all the free flowing stuff you're going to "hear," and that's the time to begin to apply your craft.**

From Inspiration to Perspiration

It shouldn't take too much reflection to realize that if God did indeed just "give" us complete songs there would be no need for further practice or development on our part; all believers would write perfect songs every time. But obviously this isn't the case. Songwriting is an art, but it's also a craft, with its own set of skills to be learned and sharpened until they are the best we can make them. The *message* may be God's; the *expression* of the message is ours. The song is expressed in our vocabulary and written at the level of our ability not His. He can certainly give us a fountain of inspiration, understanding and even revelation—but craft is our responsibility. And **Craft means knowing what to do when the great inspiration strikes.** Of course, the more of your craft you have built into your mind, the more you will create instinctively and the less rewriting you'll need to do.

◆ HOW THE SONG WAS BORN

Paul Baloche and Lenny LeBlanc: Above All

Paul had had a phrase in his journal for about two years: "Above All." One day he was alone in the sanctuary, ministering to the Lord, and a song began to take shape. It came quickly, from the heart. Much more inspiration than perspiration. Over time he took it out, visited it and worshipped with it. The verse fell into place, then the chorus built up into a great, swelling, dynamic strain, like a shout to the Lord, "All the earth will worship you, Every heart can see your majesty..." He introduced the song to his congregation, and they sang it that way for about a year. But Paul was never quite happy with it.

Paul:

I remember one time in particular that I heard people singing *Above All* in worship. I was sitting on the floor with my children, watching the inaugural prayer service for President Bush on Fox News Live. Michael W. Smith walked up to the piano and began to sing "Above all powers, above all kings..." Tears began to pour out from my eyes. My eight-year-old daughter asked, "Are you all right Daddy? What's wrong?" I replied, "Honey, these are happy tears."

I'm humbled and blown away that a simple prayer of worship, started at my little piano, found its way to The President of the United States. The possibility that this song could be an encouragement to him is such an honor.

I pray that he would draw strength and wisdom from The One who is above him...and above all. It blesses me to know that Jesus will be worshiped with this song for years to come.

One day he visited Lenny LeBlanc, to do some co-writing, and showed him the song. Paul told him, "I believe in the verse, but I feel like there's a better chorus out there." Lenny took it away overnight, and came back with a new idea. Instead of the high, celebratory lines, he came up with "Crucified, laid behind a stone..." Whoa! A total, unexpected contrast. A Paradox. It pulled the rug out from under you, and with a poignant melodic turn that nailed you in the heart. "You lived to die, rejected and alone ..." Together they worked out the ending of the song, and finished with the title line. By the time they got to "You took the fall and thought of me ... above all," they were both in tears. The revelation hit them and broke their hearts. The lesson Paul learned from that experience: *Don't take a song out of the greenhouse too soon.*

Above all powers, above all kings
Above all nature and all created things
Above all wisdom and all the ways of man
You were here before the world began

Above all kingdoms, above all thrones
Above all wonders the world has ever known
Above all wealth and treasures of the earth
There's no way to measure what You're worth

Crucified, laid behind a stone
You lived to die, rejected and alone
Like a rose trampled on the ground
You took the fall, and thought of me
Above all.

❦❦❦❦❦

Here I am, trying to write
songs about You. I think of all
the awesome, larger-than-
life words, and, really,
they just won't do.
I wondered;
have we ever
understood
what You are?
Then I saw the answer:
Yes, once, by grace, when
You manifested Yourself
in a stable in a form we
could comprehend
…and in a body
suitable for sacrifice.

❦❦❦❦❦

Jimmy and Carol

Jimmy had a life-changing moment early in his ministry. Driving in San Francisco, he heard good music of all kinds on the radio, until he got to the only Christian station, where the music was so shockingly out of date that it seemed calculated to reach a generation that had long since died. He had to pull the car over and pray. He vowed to do all in his power to make Christian music attractive to the unchurched. God opened doors for him to experiment, first in church, and later in recording and TV studios, concert halls and arenas. Carol became his partner in writing, touring and teaching.

APPLICATION:

Try some clustering. Pick a song from your greenhouse, write its title or topic in the center of a piece of paper, and follow the process we've just described.

CHAPTER 2
WHAT MAKES A GREAT WORSHIP SONG?

To be successful, any song must do two things:

1. Achieve its intended effect in the listener, by making him or her laugh or cry or contemplate or worship or whatever the song is supposed to do

2. Make the listener want to hear it again

First let's consider what makes a successful song of any kind. Then we'll examine those specific things a good worship song needs to accomplish its purpose.

The Cardinal Rule

This brings us to what we call the Cardinal Rule of Songwriting. Well—it's not really a rule. Nothing we say here is a rule. But frankly, any song that doesn't follow it doesn't do a very good job of communicating its message and probably won't get far. It 's so important that it needs a billboard, or at least a panel of its own:

> Make all the elements work together to enhance the *feeling* of the message.

Songwriting is *an emotional medium,* **a vehicle for the expression of feelings.** Think about it. If your message consists only of a series of facts and makes no emotional impact, you would do better to present it not as a song but as a list or paragraph. **Try to match the mood of the music to the meaning of the message, so the listener can** *feel* **it. This way, the song becomes more than the mere transfer of data—it becomes an** *experience.* Emotion is the soul of a song. That's why computers can't write songs. Even if they can be programmed to think, they still can't feel.

The Very Idea!

When you get an idea for a song, the first thing you should ask yourself is: **Is this idea worth writing a song about?**

- **First, is it biblical?** Because of the power of the music, the words are going deep into the hearts and minds of people who listen and sing. Nice, cozy thoughts and warm fuzzies about God are not enough; the Word of God, empowered by the Spirit, ministers life. That doesn't mean that every song has to be based literally on the words of scripture. Many fine worship songs express heartfelt devotion to the Lord without directly quoting scripture, but their concepts come out of the writer's knowledge and love of the Word. Even being biblical alone is not enough. "An omer is the tenth part of an ephah,"(Exodus 16:36) is biblical, but it probably isn't worth writing a song about.

- **Second, is it touching, moving enough? Is it something other people will care about?** Will they think, 'I've experienced that, and this song says what I feel'? Not every idea can bear the weight of being set to music.

Matt Redman: God Centered Songs

There is a call for every worship songwriter to be a 'proclaimer'— wrapping our lyrics around the deep and wonderful revelation of God in scripture. It's essential that we bring everything we write in line with the bible.

That is a challenge to be even more creative! To work even harder and search even deeper to write lyrics that stand up poetically, serve the church pastorally, and are immersed in the revelation of God in the bible. For those who have a heart to see the people of God pour out worship in spirit and in truth, and see how big a role fresh new songs have to play in that area, it is a challenge we will rise to.

Part of being a proclaimer in songwriting is to create songs which center in on God, and not on us. It's easy to fall into the trap of songs which end up being all about us. 'Meet me,' 'heal me,' 'free me' songs can be an important part of the congregational worship diet—after all, the Psalms have aspects of these cries, but if they're all that's on the menu, then we're in for some serious spiritual mal-nutrition. There's a totally different dynamic that kicks in when we honour God by writing songs that ooze with the revelation of Him, and give space to respond to that revelation.

The Right Title

A great title idea may open up all kinds of possibilities depending on the style, atmosphere and mood you want to develop.

- Right at the start, **your title should give us an idea of what *this* song is about:** "Here I am to Worship", " Awesome God," " Change My Heart O God."

- Like the cover of a book, the title delivers the first impact and whets the appetite for what is to come. Many writers begin with a title. It may take only one evocative line to set the creative wheels in motion: "I Could Sing of Your Love Forever," "Lord I Lift Your Name on High," "Shout to the Lord".

- **Try, if possible, to avoid a title that doesn't appear in the lyric.** Sometimes this is hard to do, so you just make the title as descriptive as you can and hope for the best. The problem is that people then find it hard to connect the title with the song. They may remember the song and want to hear it again, but they don't know what to call it, so they can't find it.

Jimmy and Carol:

They once wrote and recorded a song called "Discovery," in which the title word never appeared. Years later, they ran across the title and couldn't remember how their own song went.

The Building Blocks of a Song

Now, back to our Cardinal Rule of Songwriting — Make all the elements work together to enhance the feeling of the message—What do we mean by the *elements* of songwriting? **There are at least nine definable elements that make up most songs:**

The Intangible elements:

1. **Message**. Not to be confused with lyrics. Message is what you have to say; lyrics are the words you use to say it. There are lots of ways of stating the same message, some more effective than others.

2. **Style**. Such as pop, rock, country, southern gospel, black gospel, etc.

3. **Atmosphere** or ambience. A song may take us to a tropical island (as the reggae song, "Heaven is in My Heart"), or before the Throne of God ("Holy, Holy, Holy").

4. **Mood.** Not the same as atmosphere. *Mood* asks "How do you *feel* about what you're saying?" Let everything in the song tell us you are happy, pensive, sad, nostalgic, triumphant, worshipful … If you do your job in using rhythm, harmony and melody, etc., we'll feel it with you. Two songs might have the same atmosphere but opposite moods.

The tangible elements. We'll list them here and examine each of them in more detail later.

1. **Form,** the *shape* of the song

2. **Lyrics,** or *words*

3. **Melody,** or *tune*

4. **Harmony,** or *chord structure* and *voicing*

5. **Rhythm,** or *beat*

These nine elements are the building blocks of a song. Which element is most important will depend on what you want the song to do. **In a song for**

47

ministry, the most important of all is the message. All the other elements, both tangible and intangible, must work together to support it.

Hooks

Jesus said, "Follow me and I will make you fishers of men" (Mark 1:17.) As songwriters, our job is to hook people's hearts and emotions for the Lord. A fish hook catches a fish; a musical hook catches a listener.

> A good fisherman knows what kind of hooks to use to catch certain fish. Trout, flounder, catfish, and bass all require unique hooks to best capture them. Jesus told parables that his listeners could relate to and understand. He would hook them on stories about farmers and fisherman, weddings and banquets, money and mansions, and so on.

A hook is the thing that grabs people's attention and makes them remember the song. It's the part you can't get out of your head. Three days after hearing the song you find yourself humming the melody or guitar line or drum beat.

Hooks come in several varieties, such as vocal hooks (vocal sounds that aren't exactly words, like humming or wo wo wo-ing or oohing or nah nananana nah.) There are instrumental hooks and production hooks, which have more to do with playing and recording than with songwriting. But usually when we refer to "the hook," what we really mean is *the main hook line* of a song.

Jimmy and Carol:

In their Egyptian seminar, although they couldn't understand the animated Arabic discussion that followed the translation of each point they made, there was no mistaking one reaction. Accompanied by smiles of recognition, the English word "hook . . . hook . . . hook!" was echoed by one after another as the Psalms were read aloud in Arabic. The principles of good songwriting are universal, in all eras, languages and style.

In faster songs the hook line may sometimes be a little short punchy word or phrase, repeated often. In a slow worship song or ballad it's usually the most emotional line, where the longer, higher notes come together with the main thought of the message at a key place, like the beginning of a verse or chorus, or maybe the end, or sometimes both. But whatever it is, it's the thing that grabs you, pulls you in, stays with you after the song is over and makes you want to hear or sing it again.

Repetition Repetition Repetition!

Repetition is the key with hooks. It's sort of like angling for fish. The hook is dropped not just once but repeatedly. Soon it catches on and lodges in the memory.

- **The main hook will be even stronger if it *incorporates the title*,** as in "I Could Sing of Your Love Forever," "Shout to the Lord," "Blessed Be the Lord God Almighty" and "Open the Eyes of My Heart."

- **One of the strongest ways to use your main hook is to *open the song with it*.** The words, "Great is Thy Faithfulness" start the song, appear twice at the beginning of the chorus and again in the last line of the chorus. Other songs that open with their main hook are: "Lord, I Lift Your Name on High," "Change My Heart, O God," "Come, Now is the Time to Worship," "Open the Eyes of My Heart" and "As the Deer."

- **If the hook happens both at the beginning and end of a chorus, we call that *bookends*.** Bookends accomplish two purposes:

1. They strengthen the identification of the song. There's no question about what the title is.

2. They give an additional emotional punch right at the end of the song. This is especially true if they give the words a slightly different shade of meaning at the end, as in "Above All."

- Every song needs repetition, but some need more than others. **Songs to be sung *by* a crowd (congregational songs) generally need more repetition than songs to be sung *to* a crowd ("artist" songs). Highly rhythmic songs usually need more repetition than ballads,** which may be more contemplative.

The trick, though, in a very repetitive song, **lies in finding the balance between enough repetition to make the song stick and so much repetition that it gets annoying.** The simpler and more repetitive a song is, the more danger of it becoming "up-the-wall" music. This happens when the worship leader seems to have missed his exit and doesn't know where to get off. We start out in worship and end up wanting to yell "Turn the page!" as, with eyes closed, he blithely keeps us repeating a simple chorus until it brings us crashing down out of the heavenlies.

Hooks aren't something new that came in with pop music. How's this for a great example of hooks?

"*Hallelujah*" (Chorus) from *Messiah* by George Frederick Handel (1742)

Hallelujah! Hallelujah!
Hallelujah! Hallelujah! Hallelujah!
For the Lord God Omnipotent reigneth!
Hallelujah! Hallelujah! Hallelujah! Hallelujah!
For the Lord God Omnipotent reigneth!
Hallelujah! Hallelujah! Hallelujah! Hallelujah!
And He shall reign forever and ever! (Repeat)

And on it goes, compounding hook line upon hook line until it ends with the great hook line it started with: "Hallelujah!"

Hooks in Psalms

As you can see, hooks are not exactly a new idea. Now let's look back even farther—to the Psalms of the Bible. Remember, the Psalms were written to be sung not spoken. As in modern songs, some of the Psalms contain more repetition than others, but all are lyrical. Some are as loaded with hooks as the latest hit song. Take, for example, Psalm 148:

> *1. Praise the Lord.*
> *Praise the Lord* from the heavens:
> *Praise Him* in the heights above.
> *2. Praise Him,* all His angels:
> *Praise Him,* all his heavenly hosts.
> *3. Praise Him,* sun and moon:
> *Praise Him,* all you shining stars.
> *4. Praise Him,* you highest heavens ...

Eight times in four verses, we hear exhortations to praise the Lord, and twice again in verses 13 and 14. The psalm ends with the words, "*Praise the Lord.*"

Psalm 150 is a similar example: thirteen exhortations to *praise the Lord* in six verses. The psalm ends as it began, with a repeat of the principal hook line, *Praise the Lord.*

Psalm 24: 7-10 (New King James Version) is a good example of a true chorus form. Note the repetition, with slight variations.

7. Lift up your heads, O you gates!
And be lifted up, you everlasting doors!
And the King of Glory shall come in.
8. Who is this King of Glory?
The Lord strong and mighty,
The Lord mighty in battle.

9. Lift up your heads, O you gates!
And lift them up, you everlasting doors!
And the King of Glory shall come in.
10. Who is this King of Glory?
The Lord of Hosts,
He is the King of Glory.

Check out also Psalm 19:7-9; Psalm 29; Psalm 96; Psalm 103:1-5; 20-23; Psalm 107 and Psalm 109, to mention a few.

Written in ancient Hebrew, the form and lyrical quality of the Psalms survive the translation into other languages. Rather than rhyming sounds as we do, the ancient Hebrew writers made much use of metrical rhythm and parallelism, or the rhyming of meaning. In Jimmy and Carol's overseas seminars they have had their interpreters read aloud from the Psalms in their own Bibles. In European, Asian and Middle Eastern languages, it's easy, even for one who doesn't speak these languages, to hear the repetition, parallelism and rhythmic organization.

ᏒᏒᏒᏒ

What a marvel the scriptures are!
They are a blueprint for worship.
When I am at a loss for words,
I go to the praise words of
the prophets or psalmists
and read them to God,
right out loud.
What paeans of
love, acclaim
and adoration
pour out there.
I borrow their words
to prime my pump. I know
God loves to hear them again,
and I'm sure the authors won't mind.

ᏒᏒᏒᏒ

Beware the Blob

A song without form is a blob. Even a sidewalk must have a form before it's poured, or the concrete will spread out into a shapeless mess. A river's banks are the form that determines where the water goes and holds it in its course. **Form simply means the shape of the song,** whether it's verse-verse-verse-verse, (AAAA) or verse-chorus-verse-chorus, (ABAB) or verse-verse-bridge-verse (AABA) or some other combination. A song's form gives it order and cohesion, enables people to sing it together and helps them remember it. Many worship songs are just one chorus repeated over and over.

When your first idea comes for a song and you begin to develop it, you'll need to decide whether it's a verse or a chorus. What else does it need to say? Which *form* would best serve its purpose? When Paul was first working on the title song for his album, *Offering*, he thought what he had was a chorus: "The sun cannot compare to the glory of Your love…" He sang it for Rita, and she said, "That feels like a verse. When you get through singing that, it makes me want to hear a chorus." At first he was disappointed, but later he realized she was right. What he had was a verse that was crying out for a chorus to complete it. He went back to the greenhouse and completed the song.

(Verse)
The sun cannot compare to the glory of Your love
There is no shadow in Your presence
No mortal man would dare to stand before Your throne
Before the Holy One of Heaven
It's only by Your blood
And it's only through Your mercy Lord I come

(Chorus)
I bring an offering of worship to my King
No one on earth deserves the praises that I sing
Jesus may You receive the honor that You're due
O Lord I bring an offering to You

(Offering, by Paul Baloche)

HOW THE SONG WAS BORN
Paul: Offering

As I was leading worship in my church one Sunday morning, I looked out over the congregation at a certain point and noticed many people sitting down, watching the band instead of being engaged in worship. I stopped the band and pointed this out to the congregation and encouraged them not to be just spectators during our times of worship, but to be pro-active and to bring an offering of praise to the Lord. Whether it's an offering of thanks, praise, intercession, or a cry for mercy, we need to bring something of ourselves to the Lord in our times of corporate worship. I thought to myself, "We need a song that talks about bringing an offering of worship to the Lord." So in the following weeks I began to prayerfully sing out some ideas at the piano. And little by little, the song *Offering* came into being. The verses try to paint a picture of a God Who is awesome beyond our comprehension and the only way we can approach this God is through the blood of Christ and by His mercy. As we come to Him by faith, we bring an offering of worship to our King.

Common Song Forms

Let's analyze some common forms:

- **AAA. (Verse, Verse, Verse)** This is the form most used in traditional hymns and story telling songs. Each verse has different words and *builds* on the theme or story. Hymns may or may not have a repeated hook line, but the focus or subject is the same in each verse. Each **A** gives a different perspective or a deeper meaning on the subject. In story or folk type songs, the story grows as it goes along, giving us new details in each verse. The hook is usually repeated in the first or last line. It says, "This is what the song is all about."

  Examples: "Fairest Lord Jesus," "Amazing Grace," "Come Thou Fount," "Crown Him with Many Crowns," "The Church's One Foundation," "Silent Night," "Joy to the World."

- **ABAB: (Verse, Chorus, Verse, Chorus)** Each **A** is a verse, with different lyrics. Each **B** is a chorus, usually with the same lyrics each time. The verses develop the theme, and the choruses celebrate it. Each verse *sets up the chorus and leads logically into it*. The chorus with its repeated hook capsulizes the main point of the song. The hook line comes in the first or last line (or both) of the chorus. Basically it's saying, "I told you this once; I told you twice, and now I'm telling you again." It makes your message hard to forget.

  Examples: "Shine, Jesus, Shine," "Freely Freely," "The Heart of Worship," "The Battle Belongs to the Lord," "You Have Broken the Chains," "Shout to the North".

- **AABA: (Verse, Verse, Bridge, Verse)** Each **A** (called A1, A2, A3) is the same or nearly the same musically, but has different words. The hook line comes at the beginning or end of the **A** sections. Each section adds something new to the picture and deepens the theme or message. The **B** section in this form isn't a chorus, but a *bridge*. A chorus can stand alone. It states the main theme and has the feeling of coming to a complete finish when it's over. A bridge *bridges* between one A or two A's and the final A. It almost never states the core idea, but brings in fresh melodic and lyrical material that relates to it. It's sometimes called a "release," because it often goes into a different range and/or rhythm pattern, and may even change "person" lyrically (from "you" to "I" for example.) Harmonically, it usually leaves you hanging. You can't stop at the end of a bridge because the melody and harmony are not at a resting place. The tones of the chord cry out for a resolution, so it usually goes to the I chord at the beginning of the A3 section.

Examples: "Come, Now is the Time to Worship," "Majesty," "As the Deer," and the secular standard, "Over the Rainbow."

• Some songs are more extended, such as verse-chorus-verse-chorus-bridge-chorus.

"Here I am to Worship" is a good example, as is Matt Redman's "Blessed Be the Name." Others are "Forever" and "Ancient of Days."

• Some songs have a short "channel" or "pre-chorus" inserted between a verse and chorus. If the melody of the channel climbs, it's sometimes called a "climb." Duh!?

There are other forms as well, but these are the most basic ones.

Unity in Variety

In each of these forms, each line and each section *must* follow logically the line or section preceding it, informing and building as it goes. Don't just repeat the same information in a different way in each verse; develop your theme so it grows in drama or depth and power. In each form you're also looking for *unity in variety, a* cohesiveness that makes the whole song feel of one cloth, yet with different colorful touches that hold our attention.

There are many ways to achieve unity in variety:

- Use more short notes in the verses, saving the longer, higher notes for the chorus.

- Put the bridge in a higher or lower register than the A sections.

- Contrast short melodic intervals in one section with wider ones in the other.

- Make some appropriate chord changes while keeping the melody the same.

- Change the mood—try switching from minor to major for a "sunrise" effect, or vice versa to complement a sad turn in the message.

- Modulate (change key) to accentuate rising drama or depth.

- Change the key at each chorus and back at each verse? (This is rare, but surprising and effective when appropriate.)

- Do half of one *A* as an instrumental, then finish with lyrics.

If your song tells a story:

- Change time and location and increase dramatic interest from verse to verse, building to a climax.

- Go from past to present, or flash back from present to past. (This works best in AAA or AABA form.)

- Travel from place to place.

- Start with a general observation and get more particular and personal with each verse, or vice-versa.

- Introduce a new viewpoint by changing the pronouns from me to you, or I to we, etc. (But do this only at appropriate points, such as a bridge or a chorus.)

Other Song Forms

- There is a form called a ***through composed song***, which is a *logical development* of the musical and lyrical motif from one section to the next, never repeating exactly. Admittedly, the through-composed song is rare, almost non-existent, among congregational songs. The reason is that without repetition of sections, in ABCDEFG there is nothing for the listener to latch onto, just a stream of diverse sounds and words sailing by. But in the other forms the repeated sections have time to register, and the song is hammered into the listener's memory. An exception is Albert Hay Mallotte's setting of the Lord's Prayer. That works because the congregation already knows the words.

- **Many worship songs are just one chorus, repeated a few times:** Examples: "I Love You Lord," "I Worship You Almighty God," "Emmanuel," "Praise the Name of Jesus," "Isn't He?" " Something About That Name," "Lord, I Give You My Heart." If that's what your first idea seems to be, maybe you shouldn't try to make it say more. Any good song should have one basic idea, expanded on, added to, maybe celebrated by repetition.

APPLICATION:
Experiment with these forms. See how each one puts a different emphasis on your message. You'll begin to see new possibilities.

Tension and Release

The alternate building and releasing of tension, or conflict and resolution, keeps our listeners' attention alive.

- **Lyric conflict** consists in raising questions and answering them, posing problems and resolving them:

Problem: "I once was lost"

Resolution: "but now am found"

Problem: "was blind"

Resolution: "but now I see."

Problems and their solutions are not always this rapid-fire, of course. Sometimes it takes a whole verse or two to set up a problem and a whole chorus to resolve it. Not every song has lyric conflict. Some worship songs, for example, may consist of a pouring out of one's heart in love to the Lord—no conflict there.

- **Harmonic conflict** has to do with the continual tantalizing of our ears with harmonic tensions—hanging, unresolved tones that cry out to move up or down to a place of rest in the next chord.

- **Rhythmic contrast** is created by a series of short notes coming to rest on a long note, or a syncopated passage settling back into stride.

- **Melodic conflict** is a combination of harmonic and rhythmic factors. Every song has it constantly—long tones following short ones, melody notes hanging suspended before resolving to the next tone. Since melody consists simply of pitch, a component of harmony, and duration, a component of rhythm, it's hard to divorce melody from either rhythm or harmony. But conflict is what keeps music interesting—the alternate building and releasing of tension. **With too little conflict, music quickly becomes boring.**

- However, a word of caution: **With too *much* conflict, the song may become confusing and hard for the listener to take in.** Generally, too many chord changes, too many syllables and too many wide melodic leaps, all at a rapid tempo, may create a frenetic quality that can defeat your song as fast as too little conflict.

Special Qualities of a Worship Song

A good worship song shares the same qualities as any well written song, but it has certain specific characteristics not *necessarily* found in some of the others. A worship song is like a greeting card to the Lord from all of us. It speaks not just *to* us, but *for* us, providing a way to express ourselves to the Lord together. So *a worship song, more than almost any other type of song, needs to express a universal sentiment*, something we can all agree on as our own expression of love to Him.

✴✴✴✴✴

Lord, let my songs flow
out of a clean, pure,
worshiping spirit.
When Your
people hear
them, I want
them to think,
"Yes!
That's exactly
what I would say
to God if I could
write a song to Him."
Let me be the voice
of their hearts.

✴✴✴✴✴

Lord we lift our faces to You
As the flowers greet the dawn
Let Your glory shine upon us
Till the cares of earth are gone
As our hearts unfold before You
Like the petals in the rain
May the wonder of Your presence
Give us joy and strength again

(Flower Song, by Jimmy Owens)

Praise and Worship songs fall into three categories:

• **Songs sung directly to the Lord** (such as "Lord, I Lift Your Name on High," " I Love You Lord," and "Open the Eyes of My Heart")

• **Songs about the Lord** ("Awesome God," " Great is the Lord," and "He is Exalted")

- **Exhortations to praise or worship the Lord** ("Shout to the Lord," "Give Thanks" and "Majesty")

The first category is sometimes referred to as "vertical songs" and the latter two as "horizontal songs."

There are certain definable qualities that make a song effective. So it stands to reason that a list of the 25 most used worship songs would be a good thing to study. Christian Copyright Licensing, International publishes such a list, updating it regularly as churches report their use. We won't print the current list here because it would quickly be out of date, but the list is always updated on CCLI.com. Look it up and analyze the songs. You can probably already sing at least the title lines of most of them. The list changes little from year to year, but songs shift positions and each time a few drop off and new ones appear. We want to help you recognize the qualities that make these songs successful, so you can compare your own worship songs to them and see how you can improve your writing. Log on to CCLI.com.

We analyzed the current CCLI Top 25 worship songs just before we went to print, and here's what we noticed:

- **Almost three quarters of these songs are addressed directly to the Lord.**

- **Almost all are in major keys.**

- **Most of them have a "built-in cry."**

A "built-in cry" is important in a worship song. Usually this happens when key words that express heartfelt worship, longing, or yearning occur on long tones, especially in the higher register, as if reaching out or upward. See how many you can find in your favorite worship songs.

Examples:

"As the Deer." The first three syllables of the chorus stretch out in long tones on the octave: *You ... a ... lone . .*

"I Love You Lord": *to wor ...ship ...you ...*

"Breathe"(This is the air I breathe). This song has two cries, the title line with its high note on *air,* and the even more emotional cry on *I* in the first two lines of the chorus.

"Shine Jesus Shine." This cry is especially effective because the verse has been moving around with lots of short notes in the low range before suddenly leaping up to the high, open-sounding, long "Shine" on the chorus.

"Lord, I Lift Your Name on High." The chorus is full of reaching-up words.

"He is Exalted" and "I Could Sing of Your Love Forever" are other examples.

Keeping it Simple

Simplicity is vital in a strong worship song: simple lyric concept, simple melodic concept, simple chords and repetition repetition repetition. Simple, but not simplistic.

A study of the CCLI list shows us that these **successful "people songs" are simple in harmony.** A worship song with complex harmony will probably not get established. One reason is that Christian music publishers aren't interested in songs

Jimmy:
It took practically a deliverance for me to write some of the simpler harmonies in *Come Together.* In those days I preferred chords with at least four notes, and sometimes seven. (Stan Endicott once said, "I don't smoke, but those chords almost make me want to.") But I had to ask myself—Which is more important, to show off my extraordinary coolness, or to minister to the people?

Paul:

I like to consider myself a servant with my songwriting. We are servants and songs are our tools. If you really care for God's people like a true pastor longs to see his congregation built up and thriving in their faith, then you will make musical and lyrical choices that best serve the church. Regardless of how much music education and talent you have, in your writing you will always opt for what the average person will be able to sing, as opposed to writing over people's heads. It's a pride issue that we all have to deal with. Don't write music to impress your music friends. Strive to serve and inspire others with music that *they* can sing.

with many altered and extended chords that the average church band can't play. Maybe you have a diploma from the Modern Jazz Institute and a complete command of modern harmony and improvisation. Good! Enjoy it! It will help you to know how to create **beautiful and moving but *simple* colors—unexpected chord changes, pretty inversions, color tones in the melody, alternate bass tones, and colorful tones and lines in the accompaniment** —and save the more complex harmony for other occasions. Harmony doesn't have to be complex to be beautiful. That artsy side of you can do some damage. If you get too complicated you've eliminated about 70% of the churches out there that could be singing your song.

Jared Anderson
{Rescue, Beauty of the Lord}

Worship songs have one common goal and that's to help people worship. If people just think it's a cool song and you can tell that they are more drawn to the music or to you than to Jesus, then pitch it to a rock star. Not all songs have to be worship songs. If you've written a worship song, make sure it's defined by its results.

Songs for the Common Man

Mark Twain expressed the secret of his success this way: "My books are water. Those of the great geniuses are wine. Everybody drinks water."

Sir Lew Grade, a major British film producer, said, "I have the blessing of average taste. If I like it, the common man will like it." And the common man did, all over the world, as box office sales of his films proved.

Remember, when you're writing congregational songs, you're writing songs to be sung together by average people, very few of whom have musical sophistication or training. If you're a trained musician, you may have certain cultivated tastes, and it may be hard for you to lay some of them aside to create songs simple enough for untrained people to sing.

Easy to Learn

- **A worship song should be easily and quickly learnable,** or the worship service becomes an exercise not of worship but of learning. If we're asked to try and remember a lot of complicated and unpredictable changes of direction, our minds are working hard on the exercise, but our spirits are not freed up to soar into heavenly places.

This is simple human nature: we all like the feeling of success. When we find ourselves singing, almost with certainty, a new song the second time around, we feel gratified—and comfortable. If, on the other hand, we are singing a song for the fourth time and are still not sure where the next line of melody goes, we feel frustrated. And if, at the end of the song we *still* haven't learned it, we feel a vague sense of failure and probably don't want to try that song again.

- **A worship song must be not only original and inspiring, but simple, repetitive and *predictable*—Predictable to a point, but not so predictable that it's boring.** This is where a worship song differs from other songs. Too much predictability in an "artist" song might indicate a lack of creativity; in a worship song it shows craftsmanship, because a good worship song should be quickly learnable. When we hear the first two lines, we can usually predict almost with certainty where the next line of melody will go, and the next, because it sets a pattern. A bridge or chorus may start us in a new direction, but we can feel almost immediately where it's going because **one line *leads us logically* to the next. This is called *sequential writing*, and it is simply the most successful way of writing for worship songs**. By the second time through, we can forget the learning process and focus on the Lord. Examine the current CCLI Top 25 list with this concept in mind, and you'll see that the songs, almost without exception, share this quality.

- Some songs have more lyric repetition than others: "Let Everything that Has Breath," "I Could Sing of Your Love Forever" and "Better is One Day" all hammer their lyrics over and over into the memory. Not all worship songs do this, but all have plenty of melodic and rhythmic repetition, repetition of words, phrases and other hooks.

In some ways it can be harder to write a worship song than other kinds of songs, because you have to get a strong nugget of an idea condensed into a few words. This takes discipline and the art of *distillation*.

Matt Redman

Worship songwriting is not about being absolutely 'precise' or 'clever.' Often a simple little overflow of the heart is all that is called for. Simple does not have to mean shallow, and it is possible to pack some deep truth into a shorter song. Every song—whether full of words, or simple, must first and foremost be the overflow of a heart amazed by God.

APPLICATION:

We've discussed some of the components that make for a strong worship song, and there are lots more to come. Now get out some of your own songs and see how they stack up to this point. Look them over and ask yourself these questions:

• Is this idea really worth writing a song about? Would it sound honest coming from other people? Can they relate to it and make it their own?

Chris Tomlin

A song for a congregation is a unique type. I always try to keep it simple with a very singable melody. Don't leave them frustrated because they couldn't catch the song.

• Does everything work *together* to support the *feeling* of the message? Words, melody, harmony, rhythm, etc.?

• Are my hooks hooky enough? Could the song use any vocal hooks?

• Are my hook lines in the right places?

• Have I repeated my hooks enough?

• Is my song too repetitious?

• Is the title okay? Could people find the song again by its title?

• What form does the song have? Is there variety within the unity? Enough contrast between the sections? Does it all feel like it belongs together?

• Do the verses set up the chorus well?

• Does it have a built-in cry, or can I give it one?

• Is the harmony simple enough for a typical church band to play, but colorful enough to be interesting?

• Is the melody predictable enough to be learned quickly?

• •

Jimmy and Carol
Come Together

A few years ago, *Worship Leader Magazine* publisher Chuck Fromm stood with Jimmy and Carol in a Promise Keepers producer's booth, watching 55,000 men worshiping with a Praise Band. He said, "See what you started with *Come Together?*"Flattering words, but the Owenses say the worship movement was already budding when, in 1972, they created *Come Together,* the first modern "interactive" worship musical and the first ever of the big arena worship events.They had simply written songs and narration around the scriptural principles they were being taught at Pastor Jack Hayford's Church On The Way in Van Nuys, California. To their astonishment, the thing exploded in popularity.

Presented in many nations, it had its biggest outreach in Great Britain. As a result of its influence, the Archbishop of Canterbury publicly called the nation back to God, and the queen backed him in his call.

Its tour, including two packed-out presentations in Royal Albert Hall, birthed a year-long campaign by 30 troupes with praise bands and mass choirs, doing hundreds of performances, some in the largest halls and cathedrals in the nation. In Leeds, for example, 120 churches worked together to present it. Roger Forster, head of the Global March For Jesus, said, "The Marches had their start when we took *Come Together* to the streets in London." A recent leading British Christian magazine article by Paul Davis was subtitled "How One Musical Changed the Way We Worship."

Jimmy and Carol never dreamed of these results. Really, it was a thing whose time had come. All over the world, the church was ready for it. Somehow they had managed to write something that was on the heart of God. And He blessed it.

CHAPTER 3
WORDS THAT SING

What's the difference between a lyric and a poem? **A poem may be a lyric, but a lyric isn't necessarily a poem.** Take, for example, the chorus of the favorite Christmas carol:

*Gl*O *o–o–o–o O o–o–o–o O o–o–o–o O ria!*
In excelsis Deo!
*Gl*O *o–o–o–o O o–o–o–o O o–o–o–o O ria!*
In excelsis De–e–O!

This is one of the world's great lyrics, but it's a lousy poem.

Even though poetry and lyrics are not necessarily the same thing, **this doesn't mean that lyrics can't be poetic.** Look at some definitions from the Encarta World English Dictionary:

- POET: Somebody imaginative or creative or who possesses great skill and artistry and is able to produce beautiful things

- POETIC: having qualities usually associated with poetry, especially in being gracefully expressive, romantically beautiful, or elevated and uplifting

- POETRY: literary work written in verse, in particular verse writing of high quality, great beauty, emotional sincerity or intensity, or profound insight

- WRITING WITH POETIC EFFECT: a piece of writing that has the imaginative, rhythmic or metaphorical qualities and the intensity usually associated with a poem

Doesn't that describe what you want your lyrics to be? Even simple worship song lyrics, though usually not lofty, are often imaginative, metaphorical and insightful. The best writers find unusual, surprising ways of saying things.

But be careful. In trying to make your lyrics poetic or lyrical, don't lose your clarity. Don't get so "artsy" that you're out there somewhere by yourself in a galaxy far away. It takes work, but a good lyricist finds the right balance.

Matt Redman

The church needs its poets—people who somehow congregationally, biblically and relevantly translate all that's happening around them into words for the church to sing. It's a powerful thing when songwriters rise up to help the people of God to voice their response to Him. The challenge is not only to reflect what people want to and should say in a biblical way, but to do it in a language they can relate to. The aim is to use contemporary language and remain biblical and poetic. On one extreme we become too 'religious' sounding, and the other extreme too 'colloquial.'

To be a poet is to try and continually bring freshness to our lyrical worship in song. We must aim to stay on a creative learning curve, consciously not using words we've used too many times before or falling back into the same old pattern each time we compose a song. The poet is always aiming to say old things in a new way—or as Brian Doerksen puts it, universal themes in a unique way. This is part of the calling of a songwriter.

The Sound of Words

Some words just sing better than others. They ring better. They *sound* better and they *feel* better as you sing them. It isn't enough just to rhyme the ends of lines; it's important how all the words sound, especially the sustained ones, and most especially the higher sustained ones.

> ### Lyrics
> **Lyrics are meant to be heard**, not read silently off the printed page, **so it matters a great deal how they make the human voice sound.**

- **Words that make the singer sound good will also *feel* good in the singer's mouth and mask.** The long tones will ring and every syllable will roll easily off the tongue. The vowels will vibrate in the face and give a wonderful resonance to the voice.

Without clenching your teeth, hum with your lips closed. Feel that vibration? Now you've found your mask. If you don't think about this when you write your lyrics, singers may be less apt to want to sing the song, even though they may not be able to tell you why.

Vowels and Consonants

- Some vowel sounds are great on high long tones, others should be avoided if possible. Take for example the famous tenor aria "Vesti La

71

Giubba," from *I Pagliacci,* by Ruggero Leoncavallo. This isn't a song you're likely to be singing with your guitars and drums in church, but it illustrates a point. The weeping singer is pouring out his emotion on the long, ringing high notes. Note the great resonance of the *ee, ah* and *oh* sounds:

Ri - di, Pagl - ia - ccio
(Ri - di, Pahl yah - chyo)

Imagine you're Pavarotti and sing it aloud to yourself. If you can't sing that high, sing it as high as you can. Now, on those same ringing high notes, try singing "Myr-tle from Mem-phis."

Doesn't ring, does it? Certainly not unsingable, but zero resonance.

Now try, to the same tune, "Full wooden bushel." Same problem. Classically trained singers will know voice placements to get the most out of these sounds, but the tones will never have quite the sonority of open vowels. You can eliminate this problem simply by not writing these less resonant sounds on long high notes. Some vowel sounds just sing better than others, especially up high.

- No vowels sound bad, but the so-called **"pure" vowel sounds** ah, ay, ee, oh, and u, **resonate and feel better** than the short vowel sounds, as in cat, pet, sit, look and much. Of course you can't just decide to use only the pure sounds and exclude the others, because you can't communicate very well in English without using all of them. But you *can* try to use the more resonant vowel sounds wherever possible, especially on the long high notes of loud, bright songs. Some of the more muted sounds may be desirable on long high notes of quiet songs.

- **Consider also the *consonants*.** Say them aloud, not their names but their sounds:

- Some of them have length and sound softer than the others (*f, h, l, v, w, y, z.*)

- The *tonal consonants m, n* and *ng* are almost like vowels, in that they can be held out and hummed.

- The *plosive consonants,* b, ch, d, g, j, *k, p,* and *t,* are shorter. You can't hold them longer because there's nothing there to hold onto. All the consonants sound good either loud or soft, but the plosives are especially suited to strong statements.

- Some consonants can go either way: *S* and *sh,* sung loudly with strong accents, can sound like crashing cymbals: "Lightning strikes and shouts Your worth!" Sung quietly and smoothly, they sound like soft breezes.

Buzz Words

By the way, we'll occasionally throw in a few hifalutin technical terms. Don't worry if you don't remember them all. They are just handles to help us catalog and discuss the musical or lyrical devices they describe.

For instance, what is the definition of melisma?

a. smooth melody

b. poor melody

c. more than one note on a syllable

d. stomach growling

This sounds like a trivia quiz. Knowing the answer won't help you write better songs, but if you're using this book in a class, it will help your professor know if you've read the material. The answer is c. Although any two or more notes on a syllable constitute melisma, a great example of its use is the word "I" at the beginning of the chorus of "Breathe."

Two Words to Remember

- *Euphony:* the flowing together of beautiful sounds

- *Cacophony:* the clashing of harsh sounds (Jimmy and Carol call them *crash bang lyrics.*)

Here's a euphonious line, matching its sweet flowing melody: "I hear you, I'm near you."

But if you're writing a warfare song, you might want to use harsher, more warlike sounds as in Harry Emerson Fosdick's lyric from the great old hymn, "God of Grace and God of Glory":

Lo! The hosts of evil round us
Scorn thy Christ, assail His ways!

You can almost hear the hissing of the serpent and the clash of swords.

Contrast the bright, penetrating sounds of Paul's "Lightning strikes and shouts Your worth!" with the disturbed muted sadness of "The muffled drumming thudded in my heart." Do you see how the sounds match the feeling of the message? The Cardinal Rule again.

Caution: Don't go overboard with all this. Of course you can't get all the vowels and consonants smooth or hard or tonal—don't even try—you could drive yourself crazy, or at least get a severe case of writer's block; **but in your *rewriting*, try to replace words that really clang with the feeling you want to convey.**

Rhymes and Chimes

There are two kinds of rhyme:

- **Perfect or pure rhyme**

- **Imperfect or near rhyme**

One is not necessarily better than the other. Some writers prefer pure rhyme, others prefer near rhyme. Good writing can be a combination of both.

For example, one of the most common concepts in all of Christianity is love. Yet love is one of the hardest words to rhyme, because there just aren't that many pure rhymes for it. It leaves you only four options: *above* or *dove*, both mind-numbingly overworked in Christan music; *glove* or *shove*, (but how would you use either of them in a worship song?) That's about it. You don't want to make a rhyme sound trite or contrived. But there are lots of imperfect rhymes for love, like "another, enough, trust, us, run, cover, of, such, up" and many more. You won't find those in rhyming dictionaries, but they sound pleasing to the ear.

|Choices, Choices |

If you have a choice between two words that mean the same thing, choose the one whose sound better fits the feeling or mood of the line. But never say anything you don't really mean to say just to get a better ring in a syllable. It's worth working hard on a lyric to make at least a good number of the sounds and the meanings feel the same.

Imperfect rhymes can sound more informal and conversational. Let's look at some rhyming devices Paul has used in "Revival Fire Fall" (See page 77): "Fall on us here with the power of your Spirit."

- Starting two or more words or syllables with the same sound is called *alliteration*: "Pour out from heaven your passion and presence."(Three p's in that line.) The next line, "Bring down your burning desire" has two b's and two d's.

- There's also a subtle *inner rhyme* in "bring" and "burning." (Subtle in that one is accented, the other unaccented.)

- Though not an *end rhyme*, "desire" rhymes with "fire" in the next line, and also *chimes* with the long i in the same line:"Father, let revival fire fall." Alliteration here too—three f's.

- The agreement of vowel sounds, as also in heaven/presence or "Your youth is renewed" is called *assonance*, or *vowel rhyme*.

- The agreement of the closing consonants of two words with different vowels, as in "bright" and "sweet" is called *consonance*.

- And when both the beginning and ending consonants match but the vowel is different, that's called *slant rhyme*, as in *sail/soul* or *love/leave*.

- Starting two or more syllables with different vowel sounds is also a form of alliteration, as in "Open the eyes of my heart."

These are all types of imperfect rhyme, or *head rhyme*. As Sheila Davis, author of "The Craft of Lyric Writing" and other great textbooks, would say, "they create phonic patterns." They may not actually rhyme, but they make the words sing. Don't think they're necessarily a sign of laziness on the part of the lyricist. Some good writers spend lots of time purposely searching for imperfect rhymes to make their lyrics sound more natural and conversational. Some just do it instinctively, without giving it much thought, but the result is the same.

Other writers prefer to use perfect rhymes whenever possible, resorting to imperfect ones only when all else fails. **If you want your song to feel loftier, perfect rhyme may work better for you.** Perfect rhyme does have another great advantage—it's a memory device; it helps us remember lyrics. **But don't say something you didn't really mean to say just to make a perfect rhyme.**

- **Not every song has to rhyme**, of course. Especially when you're writing scripture songs, or setting to music messages that are already familiar to listeners, you may choose not to rhyme at all on the ends of lines, but you probably will use lots of assonance, consonance, alliteration, etc., within the lines, or your lyric may not sound like a lyric at all.

(Verse 1)
As we lift up Your name
Let Your fire fall
Send Your wind and Your rain
On Your wings of love
Pour out from heaven Your passion and presence
Bring down Your burning desire

(Chorus)

Revival fire fall

Revival fire fall

Fall on us here with the power of Your Spirit

Father let revival fire fall

Revival fire fall

Revival fire fall

Let the flame consume us with hearts ablaze for Jesus

Father let revival fire fall.

(Verse 2)

As we lift up Your name

Let Your kingdom come

Have Your way in this place

Let Your will be done

Pour out from heaven Your passion and presence

Bring down Your burning desire

(Repeat chorus)

(Revival Fire Fall, by Paul Baloche)

❧❧❧❧❧

"Have Your way in this place?"
"Pour out Your passion and presence?"
"Bring down Your burning desire?"
"Let the flame consume us?"
Now, wait a minute. A song has consequences.
Think about it when you write or ask the congregation
to sing it. God is going to hear those words. So, if you send
up this kind of great, hungry cry, you'd better mean it. It
doesn't do to ask for the passion and presence of the
Lord casually. I mean, what if He actually shows up?
What if He comes with His idea of revival?
There will be a cost:
major repentance;
serious submission;
death to the tender flesh.
There will be a new claim on
precious priorities—a new claim on
the entire life. The truth is, this is a song
the whole church should be singing with all her
heart. Because when the fire falls and the cleansing
is done, then comes the Kingdom and the Glory!

❧❧❧❧❧

Rhyming Patterns

You may choose to rhyme lines 1&2, 3&4. Or lines1&3, 2&4. You may try other variations, such as rhyming every line, or you might have three lines that rhyme and a fourth that doesn't. This fourth line would be your hook line which may repeat at the end of each four-line set.

- **Try to put your stronger line last in any couplet,** because your last line is the punch line and it needs to be the most memorable.

- **Maintain the same rhyme patterns in each verse** if you can, to give it cohesion. But there are successful exceptions to this, too.

Conversing With God

Most modern worship songs are informal. In earlier generations, people were more distant from each other. A man didn't call a woman by her first name until he knew her very well, sometimes until they were married, or at least engaged. God was often kept at a great distance by the use of stilted religious language. Stiff, formal, phrases such as "To Thee we give thanks, O Lord, that thou hast deigned to commune with us, thy children" have given way to warm, conversational expressions like Rick Founds's "I'm so glad You're in my life,"from "Lord, I Lift Your Name On High." That song has touched the heart of a generation as few others.

• **Rhyme the important words** if possible. Rhyme gives emphasis, and you don't want to waste it on trivial words.

Straight Ahead Lyrics

Unless you're deliberately writing in a lofty, formal style, it's best to make your lyrics move straight ahead, as they would in conversation. "To the store I will go," or "The day, beautiful it is," or "My slippers fetch me" might work okay in old timey poetry, but it's jarring in modern lyrics. It sounds like a lyric made by a contortionist. Or like dialogue by Yoda. Of course if you're writing in a lofty, more poetic or hymnlike style, or setting scripture to music, it's okay. We've done it ourselves.

Here is a good example of backward phrasing (or maybe it's a bad example) from a hymn written in 1868 titled, "The King of Love My Shepherd Is" (Even the title is backward):

The King of love my Shepherd is
Whose goodness faileth never
I nothing lack if I am His
And He is mine for ever.

Strong lyric, but we hope no one ever asked the author for directions.

The Flow of Words

Consider how your words flow together as they're sung. In an old movie called "Friendly Persuasion," Gary Cooper made a cute little bit of business out of trying to pronounce "Mrs. Hudspeth." He looked a little sheepish because he couldn't get it to come out right (Misses Hudthpeth) and he didn't want to offend her. That would not be an easy line to sing at a fast tempo. Try to say it rapidly three times and you'll see.

Sometimes the problem is having broad syllables that have to fit into little short, unaccented notes. Here's an example: Your tempo is moderately quick and you're in a shuffle pattern—dum, da dum, da dum, da dum (dotted-eighths-and-sixteenths.) Sing "On the rolling sea." Works fine, doesn't it? The syllables match the rhythm. Now, at the same tempo, try singing "On the great, broad sea." Doesn't fit, does it? The word *broad* is simply too broad to fit into that little spot at that speed. Sing your songs aloud and look for awkward singing lines. Fix them before letting your song out to the public.

You probably won't give a lot of conscious thought to all this in your first draft of a lyric. In fact, let us caution you not to. You can tie yourself in knots and bring on a serious case of writer's block by being too analytical at first. But **in your *rewriting*, see how many words you can improve by paying more attention to how they sound and feel.** With practice this will become more and more instinctive, so you won't have to do as much rewriting.

APPLICATION:

Now that we've gotten this far in our discussion of lyrics, why not get out some of your lyrics and walk through them to see if you can improve them. Ask yourself:

- Are there any unlyrical sounds I can replace?

- If my message needs smooth vowels and soft consonants, can I find more euphonious words than I've chosen?

- If my message is harsh, such as one of warfare, can I find words with crash bang sounds in them?

- Any rhymes I can improve?

- Does any rhyme sound trite or contrived?

- Does my stronger line in each couplet come last?

- Are my rhyming patterns consistent?

- Are my rhymes on important words?

- Are there any backward lyrics? (Okay in certain poetic styles)

- Is there any syllable too broad to fit where I have it in an unaccented spot, so it impedes the *rhythm* of the line?

Sensory Lyrics—Images We Can See and Feel and Hear

Like a rose trampled on the ground

Some words are bigger than others, not in their length but in the power of the images and emotions they convey: flame, consume, passion, burning, kingdoms, thrones, thunder, lightning, shining, light, glory. Words like these take us out of our day-to-day existence and into another place.

Not every lyric can make us see or feel or hear something so vividly, but when you can make it happen, it adds extra punch to your song. Let's pick apart the lyric of Paul's song, "The Way." It's full of images and sensations.

Verse 1 goes:

The way the sun breaks through the clouds
Beams of light shining all around
The way the ocean meets the sand
Waves of blue come crashing in

Then he *contrasts* these large, bright and noisy images with two close and personal ones:

The way a mother holds her child
The way You make me smile

The chorus goes:

I see You, I feel You
Like the wind against my face
I hear You, I'm near You
In every step I take
I want to follow You more and more each day
'Cause You are the way
You are the way

In verse 2:

The way the thunder shakes the earth
Lightning strikes and shouts your worth
The way the seasons come to pass
Shows my heart Your faithfulness
The way the morning star returns
The way the fire burns

This is a powerful lyric because it involves more of our senses than just hearing.

Notice also the *organization* of the lyric:

• Eight times throughout the verses Paul opens lines with "The way … ," and he uses those words to close the chorus. He also starts five lines in the chorus with the same word, "I." Starting successive lines with the same words is a poetic device called **anaphora**, and it gives a sense of orderliness to a lyric.

- Notice also the use of **parallelism**: I see … I feel …I hear …I'm near.

What if he had said, "I see you, it's you I feel?" Duh. Not only would he have lost his inner rhyme, but he would have lost the sense of unity and cohesion.

- Each verse paints picture after picture, then the chorus personalizes it: How do I feel about these things? What is my reaction? What am I going to do about it? The obvious response: I want to follow You…

 Neatly done.

(Look at him standing there, redfaced, toeing the ground and saying "Aw, thanks, guys." While we've got him embarrassed, let's embarrass him a little more by analyzing another of his lyrics.)

Here is the chorus of Paul's up-tempo song, "All the Earth Will Sing Your Praises." Look at all the devices he's used here—short, punchy lines; repetition of words, rhythms and melody; anaphora; alliteration; parallelism. The verse expands on the theme and sets up the chorus, which goes:

You lived
You died
You said in three days you would rise
You did
You're alive!

You rule
You reign
You said you're coming back again
I know
You will
And all the earth will sing your praises
All the earth will sing your praises!

Short, punchy phrases like those might seem out of place in a slow ballad, which needs long, flowing lines to achieve its effect. Either can be successful.

Ψ

One day
every voice on earth
will praise You. There will be
shouts from the mountaintops and
deserts, songs from the islands and cities,
and the whole earth will be full of Your glory.
As for me, well, I can't wait for everybody else; I'm
going to start now, so that when I do it then,
I will be rehearsed and ready.

(Isaiah 42:10-12)

Ψ

Paul's line in "The Way," "Lightning strikes and shouts your worth" is an example of ***personification***, attributing human characteristics to something inanimate. Jimmy once wrote:

I hear His thunder speak across the plain
To call the raindrops that nurse the tender grain.

Speaking of *larger-than-life pictures*, let's look at some hymns. We hear hymns so often, we sometimes forget how good they are. One of our favorites is "O for a Thousand Tongues to Sing" by Charles Wesley. Listen to the emotion of the opening lines:

> *O for a thousand tongues to sing*
> *My great Redeemer's praise,*
> *The glories of my God and King,*
> *The triumphs of His grace.*

The music builds, undergirds and lifts the words so beautifully that we begin to experience what's in the writer's heart: praise so deep that it would take a thousand languages to express it. The fourth verse is glorious, as well:

> **Hear** *Him ye deaf; His praise ye dumb*
> *Your loosened* **tongues employ;**
> *Ye blind,* **behold** *your Savior come;*
> *And* **leap***, ye lame, for joy.*

Can't you see it happening? The writer has not simply given us information; he has transmitted his emotion to us and *he has shown us something.* He has used specific, active verbs (emphasis ours) and has given us a sensory experience: we can see it and hear it.

Walter Chalmers Smith has given us some of the most brilliant picture phrases in all hymnody:

> *Immortal, invisible, God only wise*
> *In light inaccessible, hid from our eyes*

These are **big, dramatic, glorious words**—no long convoluted sentences here, just quick, explosive bursts.

A worship song by Bill and Gloria Gaither even gives us a line we can smell—it tells us the name of Jesus is "like the fragrance after the rain." A fresh and original simile.

Similes, Metaphors and Allegories

- "You are like a rose,"That's a *simile*.

- "You are a rose." That's a *metaphor*.

Similes and metaphors can help make our lyrics more vivid. The difference between a simile and a metaphor is usually found in the word "like," or "as."

The scriptures are full of similes and metaphors. The psalmists used them often: You are my high tower, my shield, my rock... Your word is a lamp ... Your word is like honey ... King David gave us a fresh perspective on our relationship with God when he wrote, "The Lord is my shepherd" and then elaborated on his metaphor.

Jesus referred to himself as the bread of life, the door... He is called the Rose of Sharon, the Lion of the Tribe of Judah, The Lamb of God…

Lots of great song ideas have come from similes and metaphors: "Like a rock,""Like a bridge over troubled water," "You are my morning star."

These next two examples by Jimmy and Carol aren't worship songs, but they illustrate the use of metaphor:

The bridge of "He Died for Us":

> *There once stood a wall, deep and wide, strong and tall*
> *There it stood, built of all our unholiness.*
> *But this Man, by His blood, broke the wall, loosed the flood*
> *Of the mercies of God to mankind.*

The bridge of "Where Have the Children Gone?" from *Heal our Land:*

Their world is full of smiling heroes
Who will take them by the hand
And lead them to the serpent
And defend them from the Lamb.

- An *allegory* is a story that uses symbolism. It seems to be about one thing but is really about another. One of the most popular examples of allegory in fiction is C. S. Lewis' *Chronicles of Narnia* series. The hero is a lion named Aslan who is really a symbol of Jesus. He demonstrates the redemptive work of Christ by dying in the place of a little boy who has broken the law. It's fantasy with a punch.

APPLICATION:

1. Find ten more similes or metaphors in the Bible.

2. Think up ten similes or metaphors of your own. One of them might start you on a song.

3. The Allegories in the Bible won't be hard to find. Jesus' allegories are called "parables."

Strong Opening Lines

Look at any list of great songs and you'll find that they have great opening lines. Follow their example and **make your opening lines as strong as you possibly can.** Don't save all your good stuff for later on in the song. If you do, there may not be any later on. Your opening line is a hot spot in your song. Paul calls it "prime real estate—ocean front property." You want it to have what realtors call "curb appeal." It makes the first impression, pulling the listener into the song. Whether or not it incorporates the title, or the main hook, it needs to be evocative. Make sure you get the opening line right, and you've won a major part of the battle.

Just the RIGHT Words

If you're a lyricist, ideas are your stock-in-trade and words are your instrument. The more fluent you are with words, the easier it will be for you to find the *right* word, which is what lyric writing is about. We once saw in a critiquing session a song changed from "pretty good" to "great!" by the subsitution of one word. The class burst into applause at the transformation. It was the *right* word. The *right* words will set the theme, the mood and the action quickly. Here are a couple of simple examples:

> ### The Right Word:
> Truman Capote, the novelist, once sat at his typewriter all day and ended up with only one word. A friend found him there and said, "Truman, you've been here all day and you've only written *one word?* "Capote replied, "Yes, but it's the *right* word."

- "Lighthouse,""sunshine,""candle"and "glory" are all words for sources of light, but each one immediately transports us to different surroundings.

- "Stagger," "strut," "dart," "glide," "sprawl""sidle," "sneak," "amble," "grovel," "sashay" and "skedaddle" are all ways to locomote, but each shows us, in one word, a different attitude.

Solomon's Wisdom

We hope this doesn't mess up anyone's doctrine, but Ecclesiastes 12:10 (New International Version) says, "The Teacher (King Solomon) searched to find just the right words, and what he wrote was upright and true." **Even Solomon didn't just write down the first words that came into his head, but *searched* to find *just the right words*.** And God included it in His inspired word, the Bible.

So involve yourself with words and ideas. Read a lot—not just song lyrics but good literature—poetry, books and articles by the best writers on many subjects. The more you read, the better you'll write. Invest in some good books on writing, or find them at the library. Learning to use words skillfully will not only make you a better writer but a more fulfilled person.

A Short Course in Lyrical Photography

Let's go a little deeper into this idea of imagery. Think of it as lyrical photography.

- *Snapshots*. You, the lyricist, are going to show us your "snapshots." *Snapshot lyrics* are lyrics we can see. They are short "picture" phrases that quickly set a scene, evoke an atmosphere, transmit a mood.

New Standards:
Famous landscape photographer Ansel Adams hiked for miles and climbed into difficult places, set up his camera and sometimes waited all day for just the right combination of clouds and shadows. One moment's click of the lens was often followed by many painstaking hours in the darkroom. But he showed us the great American west in ways we had never seen before and forever set new standards in landscape photography.

- *Fresh Camera Angles*. The problem for you here is that many of them will be pictures of things we've often seen before. After all, the subject matter for worship songs has been well picked over during the last two thousand years. There are only so many biblical phrases with which to express worship, and they've pretty much been cycled and recycled by now. So, show us some new camera angles—fresh perspectives—on these familiar themes. Give us a new viewpoint, or a new insight, or a deeper understanding of things. Every now and then someone comes up with a fresh and original expression, such as Graham

Kendrick's "Shine, Jesus, Shine!" Jack Hayford's "Majesty! Worship His majesty" or Rich Mullins's "Our God is an awesome God!", and it touches us in a new way. You can do that.

In reaching for fresh ways to express old ideas, **don't let your lyrics deteriorate into Secret Code.** There's a line in one of our favorite hymns that is unintelligible to the uninitiated. It's in the second verse of "Come Thou Fount of Every Blessing":

Here I'll raise my Ebenezer
Hither by Thy help I've come

Most congregations sing blithely through those lines without a clue as to what an *Ebenezer* is, or how it is to be raised. Actually, the second line is there to tell us what it means, but who knows that?

- *Focus.* Your snapshots may be exciting and original, but if the focus is fuzzy, all may be lost. **A song should have only one central theme, or two at the most.** You may respond, "But I have so much to say." Then maybe you have material for two or three songs ... or for a sermon. A good song will have the sharp focus that comes with knowing the point you want to make, sticking with it and developing it throughout the song.

> **Cutting Away:**
> The great sculptor Raphael was asked how he made such a magnificent horse out of a piece of marble. His answer was that he just liberated the horse from the marble that imprisoned it. In modern English, that would read, "I just cut away everything that wasn't a horse."

The question is not how many ideas can we get into the song, but what shall we leave out? Sometimes we need to be brutal with ourselves and cut away a lot of beautiful, flowery verbiage that scatters the focus of our song all over the landscape.

As we discussed in the section on hooks, your main point will be cap-sulized in the chorus of your song or in a repeated line in the A sections of a song without a chorus. Whatever form you use, remember, **your lyrics must set up your main hook by *progressing logically* toward the chorus or the hook line in every verse.** Each verse will give us new information, or a new slant on the theme, and lead us right back into the chorus. Look at any song with staying power, and you'll see how focused it is. It keeps bringing us back to the theme and socking us with its hook line. Even in the AAA form, which includes most hymns, you will stay with a central concept in each verse. "When I Survey the Wondrous Cross," for example, and "There is a Fountain Filled with Blood" never digress from their main theme, which is the crucifixion. Each verse simply expands on the theme.

Your song has a beginning, a middle, possibly a climax, and an ending. Let each verse build the mood, strengthen the theme and head straight to-ward the main hook. There should be no lines thrown in in order to make a rhyme; no irrelevant verses put there because, well, you have to have another verse, don't you?

If you have trouble sticking to the point (lyrics do take on a life of their own sometimes), try writing out the message of your song in prose, decid-ing what your main theme is and what variation on that theme you want to cover in each verse. Remember, *each verse must set up the chorus or the hook line.* If it doesn't, you've made a mistake.

- *Lights ... Camera ... Action! Action* is the key word. **Take us some-where. Show us something.** Jamie Owens Collins's "You Have Broken the Chains" takes us visually onto the cosmic battlefield and *shows* us Christ's enemies trembling in chains at the sound of His name:

Oh God, Most High, Almighty King!
The Champion of Heaven, Lord of everything!
You've fought, You've won, Death's lost its sting,
And standing in Your victory we sing:
Chorus
You have broken the chains that held our captive souls
You have broken the chains and used them on your foes
All your enemies are bound, they tremble at the sound of Your name!
Jesus, You have broken the chains!

The pow'r of hell has been undone
Captivity held captive by the Risen One!
And in the name of God's great Son
We claim the mighty victory You've won!
(Repeat chorus)

By the way, look at the rhyme effects in the last two lines of the chorus: "All Your enemies are <u>bound</u>, they tremble at the <u>sound</u> of Your <u>name</u>! Jesus, You have broken the <u>chains</u>!" The line with *bound/sound* is called a **wrap-around line**, in which the line continues on beyond the rhyme. This not only gives us an interesting break in the line-length pattern; it also places the hook/title line at the very end of the chorus (*Bookends*.) A well-crafted, powerful lyric.

> A pastor friend went to Iraq in 2003, shortly after the war, and ministered to 300 Iraqi pastors at the first Christian pastors' conference held there since the year 325 AD. He said the pastors sang "You Have Broken the Chains" together while their leaders swung broken chains in celebration of their freedom.

Paul's "Revival Fire Fall" is full of action words: "*Lift* up Your name…Fire *fall*…*Send* the wind…*Pour* out…*Bring* down…*Fall* on us…Flame *consume* us…Hearts *ablaze*…*Burning* desire."

A Good Lyric Uses:

-Words that roll easily off the tongue

-Words that resonate and make the voice sound good

-Words that feel good in the singer's mouth

-Just the right words

-Words that fit the feeling of the message.

In all the songs we've mentioned, the lyrics are streamlined for maximum impact. Good songwriters work very hard to keep their lyrics brief and, thus, effective. This is **the art of distillation**. All good writers understand it. Cicero, in a letter to Julius Caesar, wrote, "If I had had more time, I would have written to you more briefly." And C. S. Lewis expressed his admiration for the writing of George McDonald, which he described as being "weighty, economical and having a cutting edge." Economy eliminates the dross and lets the jewels shine through. This should be the goal for all writers, and perhaps for lyricists in particular. (Oh, would that it were a goal for preachers, as well.)

APPLICATION:

Look at your lyrics again and ask yourself some more questions:

- Can I make my lyrics more sensory?

- Do my opening lines grab the attention?

- Have I found just the right words?

- Is my viewpoint original and insightful?

- Does my song maintain its focus?

- Do my lyrics progress logically?

Sing your lyrics to yourself; remember, you're concerned with *how they sound* and *how they feel to the singer*, as well as *what they mean*. **Don't give up until every phrase, every word, every syllable, sings effortlessly.** This takes work, but it's what makes the difference between the ordinary and the exceptional.

● ●

Jimmy and Carol
Come Together in Belfast

 Belfast, Northern Ireland, 1973. A thousand people dead in five years of terrorism, the city an armed camp, with several bombings a day and execution-style murders. In the middle of this, the Owens family, with Jean Darnall, Pat Boone and a troupe of 50 arrived from London to join 90 Northern Irish singers in presenting *Come Together.*

For the first time since the recent "Troubles" began, Catholics and Protestants openly lined up around the block to attend a religious event together. Even though it meant a body search by British soldiers, the 1900-seat facility was jammed, and 200 were turned away.

The pall of fear began to lift when the praise songs started. A thrilling break came when a Catholic priest testified of the love he had for his Protestant brothers and sisters who loved Jesus. When the audience was asked to pray for each other in small groups, it was electrifying. A British Army major and a known IRA terrorist leader, whom the sponsors had been watching nervously, emotionally embraced and wept together. While *Come Together* was there—and for the first time in recent memory— there were no bombings in Belfast. But there had been a barrage of intercession not only in Ireland, but in England, America and even Israel. That broke the barriers and made the difference.

A generation later, while Paul was working on this book, he, Robin Mark and Matt Redman led worship in Belfast, in the largest such event ever held in Ireland! Seven thousand Protestants and Catholics joined freely together for an unprecedented night of worship.

CHAPTER 4
MELODY THAT SOARS

And now abideth rhythm, harmony, melody, these three;
but the greatest of these is melody.

(Jimmy and Carol Owens)

In the jungle of songwriting, Melody is King! ☆

(Paul Baloche)

What is there about great melodies that makes them do to us what they do? Some of them do more than just amuse us or even touch our hearts—they have a physical effect on us. We *feel* them in the pit of our stomachs. Some touch us with an indescribable longing. Others make us feel as if we're being swept away, soaring along with them. **We remember the melodies that made us feel something, the ones that took us somewhere—in short, the ones we *experienced*.**

Sing to yourself the melody of the Disney classic, "When You Wish upon a Star." Its message is the stuff of fairy tales, sung by a cricket, but its melody is a wonderful, gentle roller coaster ride—no wild thrills, just an easy soaring feeling as it glides up and down in waves. We can actually feel the lifting, swooping and dropping effects if we let ourselves go along for the ride—downhill glides that gather momentum before they swoop us back up, drop us down, then lift us up again—like riding a childhood tree-swing or coming down fast in an elevator.

Some may say, "But that's not a worship song." No, it isn't , but is there any reason a good worship song can't touch us as well as that song does? Think, for example, of "You are My Hiding Place." It takes us on a very nice ride while leading us into worship. If we could discover the secrets of songs like these and give the world a few more really great melodies, we might make it a little richer place. (By the way, "You are My Hiding Place" also has some lines of uneven length, called **"wrap-around" or "run-on" lines**, which provide a refreshing surprise.)

In Chapter Two we mentioned that in writing worship songs, we're writing for the common man. The element of music most precious to the common man is melody. Melody is what much classical music always seems to be on the brink of but never quite achieves, (which is probably why it must be supported by the government.) The common man remembers only the most melodic music. He won't recite your lyrics as he mows the lawn, but he may well hum your tune.

The Mystery of Melody

How to create melody? That's the big question. Why is it that, given any number of possible combinations of successive tones and time values, one combination may move us while others leave us untouched? No one knows for sure. This is the mystery of melody. Good melody writing is partly a creative gift. Ideally, it's a fusion of the creative and the technical; taking the creative idea and carving it into perfection. There's no fool-proof formula, but the next best thing is to have a professional-level grasp of the materials you're working with—the emotional qualities of scale tones and intervals, the shape and reach of lines. Get in the habit of analyzing great melodies. Maybe you'll discover their elusive secrets and write some of your own.

Where Do Melodies Come From?

Most of the melodic lines we write probably "just come to us." We "hear" them in our minds. As far as we know, no one has ever satisfactorily explained just how this works. The ancients spoke of "listening to the muses," religious cults and New Agers have envisioned "tuning in to the universal mind," or "hearing the music of the cosmos" or some such weirdness. Our theory is that these tune fragments that parade themselves through our minds are probably a synthesis of the music we've listened to. Just as our memory mechanism can search out and bring up past events like a computer, the music department of our subconscious is also at work, manufacturing new combinations from music we've stored there.

Sometimes it even works in our sleep. The Bible explains it this way: "A dream comes through much business" (Ecclesiastes 5:3.) If your business is music you're likely to dream music. We've recently heard of at least four major songwriters who profess to having heard at least part of a new song in a dream.

Call it inspiration or whatever you like—but it's the ability to *finish* the song that makes the difference. And that's where craft comes in. Remember our greenhouse analogy?:

Seeds (the music we hear) fall into the ground (our minds) and die (fade from our conscious memory.) They germinate in darkness. (We don't keep worrying at them.) Then one day we notice a little green shoot coming up (a motif.) We water it and nourish it (play around with it.) As it grows we shape it according to our knowledge of our craft. When it's full grown we prune it (improve it, find the *right* sounds, tones, intervals, shapes, feelings, colors, words.) The subconscious may do much of the work but rarely brings it all the way. There comes a time when conscious deliberation takes over and finishes the job. Did God give the song? Yes, but through a gestation process in the mind of the skilled songwriter. It's an organic process, *husbanded* to fruition by the artist. This is art.

In addition to "just coming to us," melodies are found in other ways, too:

- **Chord progressions.** As you play your instrument, certain chord changes will suggest melodic lines—or even lyric ideas—that otherwise might not have occurred to you.

- **The "feel" of words.** *Star Bright* suggests something quite different than *dark cloud...* Notice it isn't the sound of the words in this case—*star* and *dark* have the same tone—but the imagery that gives you the direction. A yearning or sad message might bring on a sighing, descending melody line and maybe even minor chords. A thought about the majesty of God might evoke a bowing down feeling in the melody. Celebration may call for ringing high tones or climbing melody; perhaps a switch from minor to major in the chorus to help us feel the sunrise after the darkness, the triumph after the trial.

- **The mood of your message. This may set the rhythm of your song. That will determine where you go with the melody.** If your mood is light hearted, you're probably going to move right along rhythmically, so your melody will have shorter and fewer melodic leaps to keep it singable. If your mood is serious you might want a slower tempo and some wider melodic leaps, with more emotional punch.

We keep getting back to our Cardinal Rule. Here it is again, just as a reminder:

Make all the elements work together to enhance the *feeling* of the message.

The Influence of Scale Tones and Intervals

Analyze how certain *intervals* make you *feel*. By *interval* we mean the number of scale steps from one note to the next in a melody. Some intervals have a definite character of their own and can evoke or match different moods. This isn't an exact science, of course, and can be very subjective.

> The right melodic tones and intervals can set the "feel" of your song and make your message come to life; the wrong ones may fight against it.

A good way to remember intervals is to attach each interval to a line of a song you know well and use it as a *mnemonic*, or aid to memory, until your sight-singing becomes automatic. We'll give you some of our favorite examples, but to really fix the intervals in your own mind, you might want to select your own favorite songs. Generally, in the Western world, and with exceptions, some intervals seem to have acquired the following qualities:

- **Primes** (same note): These have no particular character but are used to articulate rhythms or accommodate more syllables. However, don't knock primes—a line of repeated primes with chord changes under can definitely create a feeling. Paul's song, "All Praise and Honor," on his *Offering* album, contains a good example of this.

- **2nds**, called *step* intervals, can be beautiful and flowing, or marching dramatically around, but unless their lines are occasionally broken by wider intervals, they may get monotonous. Yet they are necessary, to set us up for the more dramatic *leap* intervals.

Example: "Happy Birthday"

- **Major 3rds and 6ths**, performed smoothly (legato) can be sweet, romantic or sentimental. We mention them together because they have similar characteristics.

  3rd: "Kumbaya"

  6th: "It Came Upon a Midnight Clear."

  However, because of its reach, the major 6th can also be a strong interval, especially if it's high and loud.

- As major 3rds and 6ths have similar effects, so do **perfect 4ths and 5ths.**

Perfect 4th. Performed quietly, it makes a purposeful statement, as in "Amazing Grace" and "I Love You, Lord." Performed loudly, the interval is very dramatic: "Here Comes the Bride," for example. Many patriotic songs and hymns of spiritual fervor begin with the interval 5—8, including two different tunes to "All Hail the Power of Jesus' Name."

"The Marseillaise" (the French national anthem) and the old hymn, "O Worship the King" each have two perfect 4ths in their first line.

Perfect 5ths can be stronger yet. They suggest horn calls, wide open spaces on land or sea or in the air or in space. 4ths and 5ths are inversions of each other and are often used together. They can evoke warfare, power, authority or majesty. They *can* be strong and martial, but they can also be very effective in gentle melodies such as "Twinkle, Twinkle, Little Star" or "I Worship You, Almighty God".

- **Octaves, upward:** a strong "unfolding" feeling, as in "Somewhere Over the Rainbow."

- **Octaves, downward:** a strong air of finality if the last leap down is to the tonic.

In evoking feeling, the relationship of a melody note to its key may be more important than its relationship to its neighboring notes or even to its chord. For instance, if a perfect 4th is from the first tone of the scale up to the 4th, it isn't particularly strong, but if it's from the 5th up to the octave, it's one of the strongest of all intervals.

- **An ascending melody line** can feel uplifting, dramatic, hopeful, soaring.

- **The *reach* of a line**—the distance from its lowest to its highest note—may often be more important to the emotion of the line than the distance between contiguous unaccented notes within the line. The fact that a line has a range of a 10th may make a stronger emotional statement than the fact that it contains a leap of a 6th.

- **The key of the song.** A half step up or down can sometimes make a dramatic difference in the energy of a song.

APPLICATION:

Try this yourself: Take one of your songs and bump it up or down a notch to find just the *right* key.

Certain *scale tones* have different emotional colors, no matter how they are reached:

- The 3rd and 6th tones of a major scale seem "sweet" compared to the others.

- The tonic and 5th are stronger.

- The minor 3rd of a major key is associated with the blues.

- The flatted 5th can feel either ominous or poignant.

APPLICATION:

These are generalities and don't guarantee success. We're just trying to stimulate your imagination. We've got you started with a few intervals; now play around with others yourself, major and minor, up and down, and see what they suggest to you. You may come up with melodies that otherwise wouldn't have occurred to you. It's a way of priming the creative pump when good ideas haven't started flowing.

The Ubiquitous 3rd

Paul and Jimmy made an interesting discovery while working together on this book. Paul was looking through a list of the CCLI Top 25 songs and remarked, "Nearly all of these songs start on the 3rd." So Jimmy got curious and researched it further. He analyzed an Integrity Music double CD worship album, containing 36 top songs, led by a variety of worship leaders. He found this:

- Twenty-two of the thirty-six songs start with the 3rd note of the scale; that is, they have the 3rd either as a pickup note or on the downbeat. Of all the 12 tones of the scale a song could start on, 61% of these songs start, or have their first accent, on that one note.

- Of the sixteen medium to fast songs, seven (44%) start on the 3rd, and nine (56%) start on a note other than the 3rd.

- None of the 36 songs start on any note other than the 3rd or the tonic or the 5th.

But get this:

- Of the 14 slow songs, 13 start on the 3rd. That's 93%!

While this is not extensive enough to be a scientific study, it does raise an interesting question: "Why?"

Our conclusion was that when writers get into a quiet, worshipful mood and begin to write a slow song, we almost invariably gravitate to the *sweetest* tone of the scale, which is the 3rd. But when we get an idea for an energetic medium to up-tempo song, the likelihood is 56% that our idea will start with a root, an octave or a 5th.

Now, armed with this information, you have two choices:

Do I want to start my slow songs on the 3rd, because that's the cream that seems to have risen to the top?

Or do I want to avoid starting on the 3rd so I won't sound so much like everybody else? Interesting question.

Building Your Melody

All right, let's say you've got your great melody idea. It's four bars long and it just came to you while you were thinking about a phrase of lyrics. The words took on a rhythm of their own and suddenly set themselves to music. Now what? You've played around with it but you're not getting anywhere. This may be the time for some deliberate application of melody writing techniques. Let craft take over when inspiration has run its course.

> Often your first idea will give you a foundational line or two and then leave you hanging in mid-air. This is where technique comes in to give you options for development.

That original idea of yours is called a ***motif***, or *motive*. There are several ways a melody can develop from that motif. **The important thing is that your melody develops in an orderly way—the second line grows logically out of the first and leads logically to the third and so on.**

Freely, Freely

Words & Music by
Carol Owens

1.God for - gave my sin in Je - sus' name. I've been born a -
2.All - pow'r is giv'n in Je - sus' name, In - earth and

gain in Je - sus' name; And in Je - sus' name I come to you to share His
heav'n in Je - sus' name; And in Je - sus' name I come to you to share his

love as He told me to. He said free - ly, free - ly, you have re -
pow'r as He told me to. He said free - ly, free - ly, you have re -

ceived: Free - ly, Free - ly give. Go in My name and be -

cause you be - lieve Oth - ers will know that I live.

About as basic as you can get are a couple of simple worship songs from Jimmy and Carol's musical, *Come Together*. The first is Carol's song, "Freely, Freely."

- The melody in the verses consists of gentle, sequential repetitions of the shape of lines, each a little higher than the one before, then descending and ending where it started.

- The melody in bar 2 of the chorus is an **exact repetition** of bar 1.

- Bar 5 is a **repetition of the *shape* of the melody** in bar 1, and bar 6 is an exact repetition of bar 5.

- Bars 9-16 are an exact repetition of bars 1-8.

This little song was the theme song of a Billy Graham International Conference for Itinerant Evangelists with delegates from 135 nations, and was translated into many languages. On a world tour, the Pope led thousands of people in singing it. After over 30 years, it still ranks high in the British CCLI list of worship songs.

Next, let's take a look at Jimmy's "Holy, Holy", also from *Come Together*.

By the way, if these little songs seem elementary, remember **one of the first questions we ask ourselves is "What are we trying to accomplish with this song?"** In this case, Jimmy and Carol wanted songs with a specific message that audiences could learn and sing together almost immediately. Things worked better than they dreamed. Both songs are sung in many languages throughout the world and are in many hymnals. Jimmy and Carol have written lots of "regular songs," with far more latitude for melodic development, that are much more satisfying to them as musicians, but none that are more widely used.

Holy, Holy

Jimmy Owens

Sometimes you can develop a melody by **inverting the *shape* of the line**.

- The first "Holy, holy" goes up, the second comes down. This is an example of melodic inversion.

- The third line goes up a little higher, the fourth comes down.

- Bars 7 and 8 imitate approximately the shape of bars 2 and 3.

These repetitions aren't exact—just close enough to create a sense of cohesion; in many cases the syllable count and other factors will differ from line to line, which adds to the variety within the unity. These are only a couple of ways a melody might be developed. Study your favorite songs for others.

The Right Key

When you're writing for congregations to sing, remember that not everybody has the same vocal range that you do. Have you ever been in a meeting when someone—usually the pastor—starts singing a worship song by himself, expecting the people to join in? There's an awkward moment when the instrumentalists are all trying to find what key he's in. Often it's a key most of them can't play. Or worse, he's not in a key at all; he's fallen through the cracks. So the piano picks him up in one key and the guitar in another, and we have a little traffic jam. Then when the song gets to the highest or lowest notes, it's out of reach of half the congregation. If that ever happens to you, we suggest you lay out until the first chorus is over; just let it be a cappella. Then have an instrument set it in the right key for the second time through. This way you'll avoid embarrassing the pastor.

- **Congregational songs must be written in *the common range*.** That's the range of the average person, generally from low B♭ up to D. You can stretch that a half step on either end if necessary, but preferably not if the notes are to be held out very long. It's demoralizing not to be able to reach the long high or low notes.

- **If a song is to have *dramatic* impact, however, it needs a range of at least an octave**—so it has room to build up to something and climax somewhere. "Shine, Jesus, Shine," "Open the Eyes of my

Heart," "Above All" and "Shout to the Lord" all have ranges of over an octave. What if your song's range isn't that wide? Then you have a choice of keys, depending on the character of the song. If it's a bright song, pitch it high to accentuate its brightness. If it's a quiet song, pitch it lower to help keep it gentle and less urgent.

- **A song with a small range can establish a quiet mood conducive to contemplative worship.** No ringing high tones, no dramatic peaks. A short chorus with simple chords, gentle tempo and a soothing melody can create a rocking, womblike comfort. Its utter simplicity helps us come as little children, leaving behind our sophistication. And precisely because of its limited range, the congregation can sing it together in progressively higher keys, to complement the rising warmth of our worship. For those childlike enough to enter in, this kind of song is a good doorway into worship. A classic example is Jerry Sinclair's "Alleluia," with its range of only four notes. Its different lyrics on each repeat allows us to linger in the atmosphere of worship without getting tired of the many reiterations of the tune. "Here I am to Worship" has a range of five notes and accomplishes much the same effect, although its form, ABABCBB etc., is much more extensive and accommodates more message to meditate on. "Heart of Worship" has a range of a 6th. (This doesn't mean that a beautiful quiet song can't have a wider range. Even "Jesus Loves Me, This I Know" has an octave.)

The "Wings" of a Song

A melody that moves rapidly needs to have its wings tucked in. Picture a sea bird with wings outstretched, soaring in lazy circles over the water. Suddenly it tucks its wings into its sides and drops like a dart, with a splash, straight into the water, then comes up, wings flapping, with a fish in its beak.

Extend your arms straight out and wave your hands up and down slowly and gracefully. It's easy, isn't it, even if you wave them high and low? Now wave them very widely and very quickly. Awkward, isn't it? It jerks you all over the place. That's what a fast, busy melody with lots of wide *leap intervals* feels like.

On the other hand, **a slower melody could benefit from wider intervals.** Not all the time of course. Most of the intervals will probably be *step intervals*, (up or down a scale step) but a slow song that doesn't have its share of wider *leap intervals* may seem earthbound. Stretch your wings a bit at slower tempos, and see if it doesn't give your melodies more interest.

The Staying Power of Great Melody

Don't let that song out of your hands until you're convinced it has the best melody you can give it. Rewrite some of your lyrics if necessary; you can say the same thing in other words if a great melodic idea takes you in a new emotional direction. We're not suggesting a lower standard for lyrics. But while some good melodies have caught on in spite of lesser lyrics, we know of relatively few lyrics, no matter how great, (except for the psalms) that have lasted without good tunes. Likewise, a great chord progression without a good melody will soon be forgotten. But a good chord progression with a great melody is a winning combination.

Rhythm styles come and go, but a great melody can go on for years. With few exceptions, the tune and its hook are what linger longest when the song is over. Melody is almost as important in conveying your song's message as lyrics; it sets the mood and underscores the emotion.

So write a melody people can ride on, something they can hum or that sounds great as an instrumental only, and as they listen, that great lyric hook you've written will automatically come to mind.

ҖҖҖҖҖ

Put an
everlasting
melody of worship
in my heart, Lord. In the
days of rejoicing, let it
ring out like laughter,
loud and clear.
In the nighttime of
my soul, let it croon
to me there, like a mother's
lullaby, until the light shines again.

Җ

ҖҖҖҖҖ

CHAPTER 5
HARMONY THAT ENHANCES

We don't intend to start you from scratch in music theory here, or to present a full systematic course in modern harmony. There's no way a book of this scope and with such a diverse readership—some lyricists and some musicians, some beginners and some professionals—could do justice to the whole subject in a chapter. That needs at least a book of its own.

To avoid boring some and confusing others, we're approaching the subject on two levels: in this chapter we'll work our way up to some fairly advanced concepts, but we'll also include an appendix at the end of the book to help bring less experienced readers up to speed. We want to share some tips that, whatever your level of experience, will stimulate you to further experimentation of your own. So we're assuming you already know at least some of the basics of music:

- Names of the notes on lines and spaces of the treble and bass staffs

- Sharps, flats and naturals

- Chord symbols

- Simple chord progressions

- Key signatures

- Note values

- Time signatures

If you don't understand these, or need some refreshing, please refer to Appendix 2, the ABC's of Music.

If you're "just a lyricist," you may want to scan through this chapter, reading the bolded points, or skip the musician talk. Or, better still, show it to your collaborator. (For a book that starts you at Square One and walks you through the music side of songwriting all the way to an advanced level, we recommend "Writing Music for Hit Songs", by Jai Josefs, published by Schirmer Books. Also check out Paul's instructional DVD entitled "Music Theory Made Easy," available at Leadworship.com)

We suggest you treat this chapter as a **"continuing application."** Read with a guitar or keyboard at hand. Play the examples and hear how each sounds.

· · · · · · · ·

The Mood-Enhancing Flavors and Colors of Harmony

Harmony, like ice cream, comes in all flavors and colors, from plain vanilla to rainbow sherbet. It can be pleasantly scented and spicy, tart, tangy, bittersweet, salty—or syrupy to the point of nausea.

Remember what we said about the sound of words evoking or matching the feeling and meaning of the message? Well, chords can do that too. **Harmony can call up all the feelings to be found in human experience**—it can make us happy, hopeful, peaceful, pensive, merry, mournful, apprehensive. It can jangle, menace, or soothe us, leave us thrilled, threatened or comforted, romantic or nostalgic. It can be pure and ethereal, lifting us to heavenly places; it can be earthy, sensual, even devilish, pandering to baser instincts.

All of which brings us back to our Cardinal Rule again: all the elements (including harmony) working together to enhance the feeling of the message.

In this chapter we want to touch on some of the harmonic devices that seem to be most used currently, and briefly touch on "modern harmony."

Tri—Tri Again

So much of the western world's music is based on the simple 3-note chord called a *triad*. "Tri" means "three" and is where we get such words as trinity, triune, and triple. Triads are the basic harmonic building blocks that serve as a foundation for most praise and worship songs. In fact, triads are the predominant chord forms that *define* various styles of music including reggae, folk, country, rock, and various hybrids of these styles. Triads are the "meat and potatoes" before you start seasoning with various spices. Triads are the blank canvas that you can put color on. Triads, by definition, are the combination of 3 musical pitches heard simultaneously: a root, a 3rd, and a 5th. If you are looking at a C scale and you play the root, 3rd, and 5th of the scale (C-E-G), all at the same time, you will be playing a "C major triad". If you start playing more than 3 chord tones simultaneously you'll be venturing off into 4-part and 5-part chords, which will automatically tell the listener that you're playing Pop or Jazz music.

Where Do Chords Come From?

There is a convenient way of notating and thinking about chord progressions without defining the key. This system has been in place for hundreds of years in classical music, and in more recent years it has been adapted using standard numbers, known as **the "Nashville number system."** Either one is correct and they can be used interchangeably. Here's how it works:

There are seven notes in a major scale. For example, a C scale is C-D-E-F-G-A-B. Each chord created by the scale is given the number of its scale step. For example, in the key of C major we have I=C, ii=Dm, iii=Em, IV=F, V=G, vi= Am, vii=Bdim

Upper case Roman numerals indicate major chords and lower case Roman numerals indicate minor or diminished chords.

The Nashville number system would be 1, 2m, 3m, 4, 5, 6m, 7dim. To use this language we would say something like "let's play a two minor chord, then go to the five chord for two beats, then back to the one chord."

The major scale pattern we described above is the same in any key. If you build your chords from a major scale, the pattern will always be Major, minor, minor, Major, Major, minor, and diminished. Here are a few examples:

I	IV	V	I
C	*F*	*G*	*C*
D	G	A	D
F	B♭	C	F

These would be called a "one-four-five" progression. Even though the keys are different, the effect of the progression is the same in each case.

Learning the number system will enable you to communicate more effectively with other musicians and help you understand why certain chords and progressions work and feel better than others. Another advantage is that if you write your progressions in numbers and discover that the key is too high for you to sing in, it's easy to move it to another key without having to rewrite all of the chords again.

All of the chords derived from the major scale will have a sense of belonging to the "tonality." Think of them as working together as a family regardless of the key. These "family" chords are called diatonic chords. I, IV, and V are always major chords and ii, iii, and vi are always minor. Any chords in a progression that aren't part of this pattern are called non-diatonic chords. They are the exceptions. The "seven" chord is rarely used in popular music and usually substituted with an inversion of the "five" chord using the seventh degree of the scale as the bass note. (More about inversions to come.)

Let's look at some common progressions using the number system.

I-IV-V: *1-4-5*

Many popular choruses utilize this simple progression or some slight variation of it: Examples are the A sections of: "Lord I Lift Your Name on High," "The River Is Here," "Lord Reign in Me," "Forever," " I Can Only Imagine," "Heaven is in My Heart," "Step By Step," " Shout To The North," "Let It Rise," "Better is One Day," "Every Move I Make," "You Have Broken The Chains," "Let The River Flow."

I-vi-IV-V: *1-6m-4-5*

Besides being the classic 50's doo wop progression, this pattern has thousands of popular songs based on it, including many well loved choruses: "I Will Celebrate," "My Life is in You," "Jesus, Name Above All Names"

I-V-vi-IV: *1-5-6m-4*

"In The Secret," "I Will Not Forget You," "Hosanna," "Rise Up And Praise Him," "Lord, I Give you My Heart" and the beginning of "Shout To The Lord"

I-IV-vi-V: *1-4-6m-5*

"Trading My Sorrows"

I-V-ii-IV: *1-5-2m-4*

The Chorus of "God of Wonders" and the A sections of "Light The Fire Again" and "Come, Now is The Time To Worship"

I-ii-IV-V: *1-2m-4-5*

"I Could Sing Of Your Love Forever" and "Humble King"

Inversions

A basic triad has three notes, 1-3-5 or 1-♭3-5 (G-B-D or G-B♭-D). Most of the time they are played in what is called "root position."

An inversion is a chord whose root is *not* the lowest note. A *first inversion* is when the 3rd of the chord is on the bottom. For example, G-B-D becomes B-D-G. First inversions are used a lot in descending or ascending chord progressions and tend to have a majestic or anthemic quality about them. See Jimmy's anthem, "If My People Will Pray," page **129**. The same with *second inversions* where the 5th is on the bottom. G-B-D becomes D-G-B. Inversions are usually notated as *slash chords,* with the bass note written below or after the chord: G/B or D/F#. Other songs that have a lot of inversions in them include "He is Exalted," "Above All," "Here I Am To Worship," "Shout To The Lord," "The Potter's Hand" and "There is None Like You."

Take the time to play through these songs and notice how the inversions create emotion and drama. Now try playing the same songs without inversions using only root postion chords. Wow! What a difference. Inversions can wake up a simple three chord song and turn it into an anthem.

Compare the following progressions on the piano or guitar.

G	C	D	G
G	C/E	D/F#	G

Feel the difference?

You haven't really written a chord chart until you've designated what the bass notes are. (We don't mean all the notes a bass player will improvise, just the bass note of the chord.)

If the bass note is a tone not appearing in the chord, it's called an **alternate bass note**. The E chord with a 7th in the bass (E/D), for instance, is quite a different animal from the E7th chord. Play it:

D / / / | E7 / / / | D / E / | A / / / |

What's wrong with that? Nothing. But now play it again, substituting E/D for that E7 in bar 2. Same notes, but stacked differently. Do you feel that extra tension and richness?

Spend some time playing some of *your* song ideas. Try putting the 3rd or 5th in the bass and see if it doesn't take your song to a whole new level. Developing an ear for inversions will broaden your harmonic horizons.

Why "Modern" Harmony?

"Modern" harmony probably got its name from the fact that it contained concepts that hadn't been commonly used before. It started when someone got the idea of stacking up a notch on top of the triads (three-note chords) to become 7th chords, or tetrads. These were a bit daring to the unaccustomed ear, but with usage they became familiar and led pioneering spirits to move onward to 9ths and 11ths and 13ths, with various kinds of alterations and added color tones. Then they ran out of growing room: the next notch in the stack of 3rds would have been the 15th, which of course is the same tone as the tonic, so there was nowhere left to go. Styles have changed over and over and different chords and color tones have come and gone in popularity, but all songs still draw from the same pool of harmonic resources. Nearly anyone can make up a song with three or four triads. But we want to stimulate your creativity to paint more richly from the palette of harmonic colors to make both your music and your message more vivid.

Color tones are the spices of music. These are any tones other than the common working tones of the chord, which are 1, 3, 5, and the (lowered)7 in a dominant 7th chord. The color tones are:

• Added: 6ths, major 7ths, 9ths

• Suspended: 4ths or 2nds in place of 3rds

• Extended: 9ths, 11ths, 13ths

• Altered: such as diminished or augmented 5ths and 9ths and augmented 11ths.

A Call to the Colors

✓ The faster a piece of music moves the less need it has for added harmonic (or melodic) color. Excitement can be generated through rhythmic intensity alone, especially if you're doing traditional rock 'n' roll or pure country. But in contemporary pop-style music at medium to slow tempos, we have an opportunity to enhance the music with more color.

We aren't saying pure triads can't be beautiful—much great classical, folk and pop music and nearly all worship songs have been written that way. But it's the trite, overused progressions of triads, the monotonous, machine-like bass lines with too many roots and 5ths, that can become insipid. We aren't suggesting that you use color tones in every chord—sometimes the "right" chords are pure, unadorned, ringing triads—your ear will tell you. **The idea is not to toss colors around indiscriminately, but to know how to use them effectively to enhance the music and the message when it's appropriate.** We'll show you some examples.

Get 'Em While They're Hot

Times change, and so do fashions in music. Every now and then a different harmonic device enjoys its turn at bat, in time becomes commonplace, grows into a cliche and eventually falls out of favor because of overuse. It needs a rest for a while, sometimes, it seems, for a period of even a few decades. Then a new generation discovers it, as though they had found something new, and off it goes again. Here are a few examples:

- *The major 6th chord*, very popular in music of the 1930's and 40's, **is for the time being little used,** except in passing, (although the 6 and 9 added together to a triad make for a beautiful chord.)

- *Augmented and diminished triads* aren't heard much these days, unless they're passing quickly through a progression, although the diminished 7th chord is still a valuable tool in some styles.

- *The major 7th chord.* It hasn't been too many years since this chord was heard nearly everywhere in dreamy pop ballads, but now it's used more sparingly, and rarely on the end of a song. Because it keeps the ear from coming to a complete rest on a pure triad, it lends the music a wistful, nostalgic quality.

But in recent years the major 7th chord has been making a comeback, this time in a different way. It's being used in an aggressive alternative style of music. Listen for it in bands such as *Coldplay* and *Switchfoot*. And check out the opening major 7th chord on Paul's "My Reward."

- **Much pop harmony today, including a lot of praise and worship music, is mostly *triadal*.** But simple doesn't have to mean boring. You can use an unexpected triad or a pretty inversion. Or you can add one tone to a triad, such as a non-triadal melody tone or an alternate bass note, and give it more color.

- **The color tone of choice today seems to be the added 9th.** In major it has a ringing beauty, in minor it's even more dramatic.

The added *9th?* Why don't we just call it the "2"? We're getting to that. (If you're an advanced musician, please just bear with us a moment while we bring everybody up to speed. This is an important point, and even some professionals don't always agree on this distinction, which can lead to confusion.)

Remember, a scale is 1 through 8. When you get to the octave (8), you start over with all the same notes. 1 and 8 are the same note, 2 and 9 are the same, 4 and 11 are the same, and 6 and 13 are the same.

G A B C D E F# G A B C D E F# G

1   2 3 4 5 6 7   8 9   11   13

Make sense?

So … If the "2" and the "9" are the same note, why then don't we simply call it the "2"? Good question. It's a technicality: **A "2" chord and an "add 9" chord are similar, but not the same.** Here's the difference:

When you see the chord symbol G2, that implies that you are going to play the "2" *instead of* the 3rd, or "3" of the chord. The third of any chord is what determines if it's a major or a minor chord. So when you play a "2" *instead* of a "3rd", you create a mysterious quality that sounds neither major nor minor. Cool, huh?

On the other hand, an "add 9" chord implies that you are going to play the entire triad *and* add the "9" note. These two chords have quite a different personality from each other.

1. Let's try adding the 9 to our triads. Starting with the G chord, add the "A" note. Play the chord and get acquainted with the "quality" of the "add 9." Sometimes we rush through our chords in a song and we never stop long enough to smell the roses or in this case, "feel" the emotion. Listen to the chord again. No, we mean it. *Really* listen. Isn't that a beautiful chord?! Just by adding the "9", we get a completely different quality. How would you describe that particular color? Bright? Mellow? Sweet? Ambiguous? Go ahead and play each of your basic triads and then practice adding the "9".

2. Now play the G triad with the "A" *instead of* the "B" note. That's a "2" chord. Hear the difference? Play all three chords, the triad, the add 9, and the 2.

- **Experiment with adding the major 7, 11, or 13 to some of your chords**, but don't get carried away. Colorful as they are, it's dangerous to add too many colors to our songs unless we're are aiming for jazz worship music. One well placed add 9 chord or major 7 chord can add far more than a dozen distracting voicings.

- *The 3rd is sometimes omitted* for a strong triumphant effect. The chord has an open feeling with the sweetness of the 3rd removed. You can hear this sound a lot in the music of the band U2. A lot of our modern worship music has been strongly influenced by U2. You can call this chord either a "no 3" or a "5" chord (e.g. E no 3, or E5.) Think of these chords as electric Celtic music.

- This next point is not new, in fact it's centuries old, but some musicians don't seem to realize that if you have a 3rd in the bass, it sounds better to omit it in the upper harmony, unless it's two or more octaves from the bass.

- The *Picardy 3rd*. This is another centuries old idea. It happens when you play a song in a minor key but end it on a major chord, as in "Greensleeves," (attributed to Henry VIII, the first monarch to tour as lead singer with his own band.) Greensleeves is also known as the Christmas carol, "What Child is This?" But if you use this, be careful what your message says. The Picardy 3rd brings a ray of sunshine right at the end that says, "Song's over. And they all lived happily ever after. Problem solved." But if your message leaves your listeners with an unresolved problem to ponder, best end it on the minor chord instead. The Cardinal Rule again.

- *The dominant 7th chord*, **with its variations, is simply the most active chord of all.** It demands to resolve, and it's so versatile it can resolve to almost any chord. It can resolve down a perfect 5th or up a perfect

4th, or down a half step, or up or down a whole step, or up or down a 3rd, to any chord, major or minor, built on that tone. But the pure V7 has been used so much that many pop musicians today seem reluctant to commit themselves much to it. Let's say for example that we're ending a phrase with the progression V-I, one of the most common in music. It's heard constantly in three-chord music, such as Southern Gospel, Barbershop, Black Gospel, Blues and Rock 'n' Roll. But in pop-style ballads some musicians do various things to keep away from it, or to minimize the time they spend on it:

1. They may temporarily evade the V7 by going first to the "dominant of the dominant," usually a iim7, then to some form of the V7.

2. They may hang onto a *suspended* V7 (with the 4th instead of the 3rd) for a while before sliding down to the 3rd, then resolving to the next chord. As often as not they don't slide down to the 3rd at all, but just resolve directly out of the V7sus4 into the next chord, which is usually the I chord or other chord with a tonic function, but may be a surprise chord. As we said, the dominant 7th can resolve to almost anything. The dominant 7th chord, by the way, which in more traditional harmony was limited to the V7, nowadays theoretically can be built on any tone if it feels comfortable in the context of the style.

3. (Remember this for later, in our discussion of non-diatonic chords and substitutions:) They may also insert some form of a ♭VII chord in place of, or before the V7.

4. Or . . . they may do all of the above, or some other tricks as well.

• **A very versatile chord is the IV/V** (pronounced *"four over five"*), much used today in place of the V7 for turnarounds. It sounds like a

125

V9sus without its 5th and resolves easily to the I or any other chord the V7 might resolve to.

- Here's a chord we want to call particular attention to: **The *subdominant minor 6th* (ivm6)** is the most striking of the subdominant minor chords (chords that contain the lowered 6th of the key.) You can find more emotion in this chord than in just about any other. Jai Josefs, in his excellent book, "Writing Music for Hit Songs," describes this chord as"poignant," " wistful," " nostalgic," " emotional" and "bittersweet,"and we find it, indeed, to be all of the above. The Beatles used it a lot and now bands like Coldplay are sneaking it into their songs. Listen for it, too, in David Gates's haunting standard, "If." (That song, by the way, is worthy of special study. That half-step descending line through the middle of the harmony might set you in the proper mood to write a worship song of deep meditation and adoration.)

- A device much used in playing and arranging now is *pedal point,* or long tones—seeing how long a string pad, for example, can stay on one note, or two notes a 4th or 5th apart, bar after bar, while the chords change to and fro around them. This is very nice in slow ballads, lending a flowing linear quality to the texture and adding constantly changing colors to the chord line.

- A pleasant sort of momentary tension can be effected by hanging a whole triad above the bass tone of the target chord, then resolving down, as in the G/F—F change on "*might-y*" in "Blessed Be the Lord God Almighty." You can also hear this device on the verses of "Above All" when singing… "above all *pow-ers…*" "above all *na-ture…*"

Chord Functions and Substitutions

There are three basic types of chord functions: tonic, dominant and subdominant.

- A chord with a *tonic* function feels at rest. You could play it on a piano and walk away from it feeling fulfilled. Basically, the I chord (based on the first note of a scale) is called the tonic. But the iii and vi chords, though not as restful as the I, also have a tonic function and can be substituted for the I chord.

> Beethoven's wife once got him out of bed by playing a dominant 7th chord on the piano. He lay there and took it as long as he could, then jumped up and played the resolution to the tonic chord.

- A chord with a *dominant* function feels as though it needs badly to resolve to a place of rest. Thus it creates motion. The V chord is called the dominant. The viim7b5, though rarely used today, is also dominant in its function.

- A chord with a *subdominant* function is sort of in between—you want to hear it resolve but you feel no great urgency for it to do so. The IV chord is called the subdominant. The ii chord has a subdominant function and can be used in place of the IV.

Chord progressions consist of an interplay between these three types.

Basic Chord Substitution Chart

In place of	You can use
I	iii minor or vi minor
IV	ii minor
V	vii diminished or bVII

- Technically, any chord can be substituted for another with which it shares a common tone. But to be realistic, not every chord *sounds* right in every situation. Let your ear be the final arbiter when you're making chord substitutions.

Why do we substitute chords? Mainly for color, for spice, for variety, sometimes to match the feeling of the words better. Let's say you've written an eight-bar A section and now you've writing the next A section with the same, or nearly the same melody. To create more color and interest, you change a couple of chords by substituting other chords that have the same function. The result is a new and fresher sound instead of just an exact repeat of the previous section.

Example:

Basic Progression: |C / / / |F / / / |G / / / |C / / /|

Substitutions: |Am7 / / / |Dm7 / / / |Bb / / / |C add 9 / / / |

Non-Diatonic Chords

Unless we're jazz musicians, it may be easy to stay limited in our harmonic creativity by using chords and melodies built only on the scale of the key we're in. But non-diatonic chords can add beauty and pathos to our music. We're not talking about something avant garde or weird sounding. It can be very simple, logical and natural sounding. Play for yourself the music to Jimmy's anthem "If My People Will Pray," and study the chord progression. Note that the chords in bars 3, 5, 11, 12, 13,

Stretch your Creativity

Stretch your creativity by letting your melody grow into new directions, stepping outside the key and working your way back in.

If My People Will Pray

Jimmy Owens

14 and others are non-diatonic. This progression grew out of experimenting with a descending chromatic bass line, which took on a life of its own and got Jimmy off into some chords he probably wouldn't have thought of without it. These in turn gave rise to a melody line that might not have occurred to him apart from the harmony.

- The most commonly used non-diatonic chord is probably **the ♭VII chord,** built on the flat 7th of the scale. It's often substituted for, or leads into, the dominant (V) chord. Some examples would be just before the choruses of "Shout To The Lord" and "Shine Jesus Shine" where it goes "…never cease to (♭VII) worship You" (V) and (♭VII) "shine on (V) me." The ♭VII chord works well in a dramatic or serious passage, but be sure you consider the lyrics at that point before you use it arbitrarily; it may change the tone of the message, because it lends a kind of gravitas, or seriousness, that the ordinary V or V7 lacks. The ♭VII chord is also used to create a classic rock or blues kind of feeling. Sing along with David Ruis's "You're Worthy of My Praise": (I) "I will worship… with (♭VII) all of my heart…and again with "I will lift up… my (♭VII) eyes to your throne."

- Another commonly used non-diatonic chord is **the ♭6maj, or ♭VI.** It's a very dramatic chord used to give an anthem-like quality to your song. Remember the classic "To Him Who Sits On The Throne": "Be (♭VI) blessing and glory and (♭VII) honor and power for (I) ever"

It's an effective device to take your song to a completely different place as in the bridge of Don Moen's "God Will Make A Way."

Less is More

If you use modern harmony, keep your chord designations as simple as possible. For example, you almost never see an 11th chord, unless the

11th is altered in some way. The reason is that there is a simpler way of designating the 11th chord:

Technically you could call Example a a C11 (missing its 3rd, to keep from becoming too dissonant. In this key (F major) it's a V11, but hardly anybody ever calls it an 11th chord, because it's easier to consider it simply a Gm7/C, or iim7/V (Example b). If you're working with less experienced musicians, there's an even simpler way to get almost the same effect. (Example c). If you omit the G from that chord, what do you have left? A Bb triad over a C in the bass, or IV/V (four over five,) that nice turnaround or modulating chord we mentioned earlier. Your ear will probably be just as satisfied with or without the G. Sometimes in jazz it's necessary to spell out very complex chords, but if there is an easier way to do it, use it.

What About Minor Harmony?

Our discussion so far has only dealt with major keys but there are many popular songs that employ a minor key center. It's interesting to note that most of the "minor" songs that have become standards in the church begin in a minor feel, then change to a major key feeling on the chorus. Examples include "Awesome God," "The Battle Belongs to the Lord," "Praise Adonai" and "More Love, More Power." Most pop or western forms using a minor scale are based on the harmonic minor scale. In E minor, that would spell: i (Em), III (G), iv (Am), v (Bm), VI (C), VII (D) Notice that the songs below utilize every chord in the harmonic minor scale, except one. The missing one is the ii, which is seldom, if ever, used.

Awesome God:

The Verse Contains: Em Am Bm C Bm

The Chorus Contains: C G D Em Am Bm

The Battle Belongs to The Lord

Verse: Em Am Bm

Chorus: G D C Am Bm Em

More Love, More Power

Verse: Em Cmaj7 Bm7

Chorus: Am7 Bm7 Em Cmaj7

In the key of A minor the chords would be:

i (Am), III (C), iv (Dm), v (Em), VI (F), VII (G)

Praise Adonai

Verse: Am F C G

Chorus: F Am G Dm

Minor chords put out a lot of emotion. There is usually an intensity or urgency communicated. A cry of the heart. Look over some of your own song lyrics. Are there any that might fit a minor chord feeling? Perhaps you have a worship song that sounds "too happy" or "campy". Try singing your same melody over a new set of minor chords and see if it doesn't change it for the better. A lot of the 'alternative rock style' that has spilled over into the church employs the emotion of minor keys. Be careful though. Too much minor harmony can get depressing and heavy. Use minor keys like a fine spice. Sparingly.

Surprise!

It's refreshing to hear a well-placed surprise chord. Of course, they need to be used sparingly, or they aren't surprising, and you need to be careful how you use them in a congregational song. But they work just fine in a congregational song so long as they don't change the melody. Listen for example to the last chord in each chorus of "Praise Adonai," on Paul's *Open the Eyes of My Heart* album. You were expecting a C major chord, weren't you? But that Bb chord against a C in the melody makes it feel like the ground has dropped out from under us and left us floating in a momentary out-of-body experience.

What to Leave Out?

Before we move on, this raises another question: When we have a chord with more different tones than voices, which notes do we leave out? Well, we need the 3rd because that tells us whether the chord is major or minor. The altered, added or extended tones are important to give the chord its flavor. There is no absolute rule, but if we play around with the voicing, our ears will probably tell us that the two notes that are expendable are first the 5th, then the root. There are probably exceptions to this. Play it and do what sounds good.

Changing Keys

There are many ways to modulate, or change key. Some are imaginative, surprising and inventive; others have been used so often they have become cliches.

- Some modulations are not really necessary to the song, but they enhance the arrangement, such as doing the last chorus or two a step or half step higher. These are called *arranger modulations*, as opposed to *composer modulations*, which are integral to the structure of the song.

- Whatever purpose the modulations serve, they all boil down to two categories:

- The more common of the two is the *pivot chord modulation*, in which the new key is approached by a chord common to both keys.

- A *direct modulation* is a change into a new key without using a common chord. One way to modulate directly is simply to start the next chorus or verse in the new key with no modulating chord. This can be startlingly effective in a "presentation" song, (that is a song sung to but not by the audience) but is not recommended in a congregational song because most of the congregation doesn't know the key change is coming until it has already happened. They suddenly realize the train has gone onto a new track without them, so they drop out and come back in when they've figured out where the melody has gone. Thus we have a momentary train wreck. It isn't as though we have come crashing irreparably down out of the heavenlies, but our worship has been at least momentarily side-tracked.

Having said that, we must admit that for every principle we point out here, you can probably find at least one example of where somebody has done it the other way successfully. That's why we say these are not rules but principles. Darlene Zschech used a direct modulation with striking effect in her own recording of "Shout to the Lord." Once they've learned to expect it, the congregation is laying for it with relish, and it gives a great lift going into the last chorus.

- **The most common modulation of all is going up a half-step or whole-step by using the unadorned V7 chord of the new key to**

introduce the next verse. This is okay, even expected, in certain traditions such as Country or Southern Gospel, but if you're writing in a contemporary style and trying to be a bit imaginative, you might want to explore some other avenues instead.

- The problem is that in a congregational song with a fairly broad range, anything beyond a step up may stretch beyond the comfort range of half the congregation. But there are solutions. **One way to modulate is by use of an instrumental interlude.** The modulation can begin anywhere in the interlude, at the beginning, even in the middle of a measure, and by any imaginative modulating device you choose. You can even get a refreshing lift by doing the interlude in any other key, even half an octave away, then modulating into the new vocal key before bringing the congregation back in. Even if you modulate back into the original key, it will feel like a new key when the singers come back in.

- We mentioned earlier the versatility of the dominant 7th chord and its ability to resolve to almost any other chord. This makes it very useful in modulating. You can modulate in a surprising way by resolving a dominant 7th chord to an unexpected chord and establishing a new key.

For example, try this progression: You're coming up to the end of a chorus in A major and your last three chords are A E7 A. That's one of the most common and overused progressions in all of music. But you want to give the song a dramatic lift, so you go: A E7 F! The F chord becomes the downbeat of a new key (F), an instrumental solo takes off and rises from there, and you find yourself soaring along in a new *key a minor 6th higher!* It can feel like you're being launched into orbit.

• Another great example of an unexpected modulation is found in George Harrison's "Something." There's an electric guitar solo line at the close of a verse in the key of Cmajor. Again, the next to last chord is a V, leading to a I chord. Everything in the listener's western upbringing has prepared her for that V chord to be followed by a I chord. But the second time around, instead of a I, it's a surprise chord, and not only a surprise chord, but a surprise modulation. The whole dominant triad slides upward a whole step in parallel, to A, and we find ourselves riding along in a new key *a major 6th higher*. This is a direct modulation. There was no hint in the harmony that it was coming. As we mentioned above, don't try a direct modulation that changes the melody while the congregation is singing. Let it be an instrumental modulation, or you'll have a train wreck.

• **A diminished 7th chord** is also a very versatile modulating chord, although not appropriate in every style. Its tones are all equidistant, a minor 3rd apart. In the key of C, for example, if it's built on the leading tone (the 7th of the scale) the notes are B, D, F, A♭. The next step above that brings you back to B, the note you started on, and if you keep repeating the cycle, it feels like a ball rolling over and over, either uphill or downhill. The chord can resolve easily to any one of eight chords, the root of each a half step up from one of its tones, in either major or minor. Be careful how you use it, though, because it may be uncharacteristic in some styles, even as a major 7th would be out of place in the blues. It's used more in classical music than in pop but is often found in certain styles such as Black gospel and 1920's happy pop music.

• Sometimes we change key for just three or four bars and then resolve back into the original key. In this case we usually don't bother to change the key signature, but use accidentals during the excursion. A change of key is not really considered a modulation unless it stays in the new key long enough to become established as a new tonal center.

We hope we've stimulated you to further experimentation on your own. Keep listening and be alert for harmonic ideas that are new to you. When you hear something on a recording that strikes you, analyze it to find out how it was done, then use it to freshen up your own music.

Have Fun

There are lots of ways to modulate. Master the common ones, then have fun finding fresh and interesting ways to do it. The possibilities are many, and you may discover some delightful surprises.

ℑℑℑℑ

Father,
You choose the song;
I'll find the page.
You sing the melody;
I'll sing the harmony.
You choose the tempo;
I'll march to Your drum.
Help me to listen and get my part right.
Then we can make beautiful music together.

ℑ

ℑℑℑℑ

• •

Jimmy and Carol
If My People

The *Come Together* presentation in explosive Northern Ireland had been covered by intercessory prayer. The result: no bombings in Belfast for the first time in five years. Jimmy and Carol took note. Days later, a national pastors' conference in England focused on II Chronicles 7:14, where God promised national healing if His people would humble themselves and pray. The same word came from Billy Graham, Bill Bright, Pat Robertson, Jack Hayford and others. The Owenses felt the Lord urging them to study those scriptural principles and write them into another musical event: *If My People.*

Thirty thousand attended its Los Angeles area premieres. In Britain those *Come Together* mass choirs took on the new musical, and again churches, halls and cathedrals were filled all over the land. The Church of England and Catholic archbishops jointly presented four events in Westminster Cathedral and two in the Albert Hall. Protestants and Catholics again united in Ireland to pray together for their nation.

In 1975, at Jimmy's proposal, the first Summit Conference of Church Leaders in America unanimously called for the first Friday of each month to be observed as a day of fasting and prayer for the nation. During 1976, the U.S. Bicentennial Year, a 70 city national *If My People* tour saw many thousands commit themselves to pray regularly for America. Following the musical, Jimmy taught pastors on national intercession, and Carol and seven other well known Bible teachers followed with prayer seminars. The monthly day of fasting and prayer died down after the Bicentennial year, but has since picked up steam and spread to many nations. (See www.Intercessors for America.org, for how you and you and your church can be involved.)

If My People's sequel, *Heal Our Land,* which they created in the mid-1990's, has had many presentations in the U.S, including some 40 city-wide events, as well as in some other countries.

CHAPTER 6
RHYTHM THAT MOVES (AND OTHER CONSIDERATIONS)

Rhythm—the Groove and the Feel

Rhythm is the heartbeat of music. It has much to do with establishing your song's mood and atmosphere. **Rhythm is motion, and the feel of the motion should correspond to the feel of the words, to bring life to the meaning of the message.** A gentle message calls for a gentle beat. A strong message may need a strong beat. **Any song needs** *energy*. Even a quiet song needs a quiet intensity, and rhythm is the pulse, the heartbeat, that keeps music alive.

Several terms have to do with rhythm, some of the most common of which are *tempo*, *rhythm pattern*, *groove* and *feel*. Some of them get interchanged, but they don't all mean exactly the same thing. (If someone has a different concept of what some of these terms mean, we won't argue. Some are pretty loosely defined. But for the purposes of our discussion, we'll use these definitions.)

- *Tempo* simply means the speed of the music, as measured by a metronome—so many beats per minute, or by indications such as "slow, moderate, fast," etc. There are Italian musical terms to define tempo, but this is an informal course, so we'll stick to English.

- A *rhythm pattern* tells us not only how many beats there are in a measure, but also where the accents fall, as in One and <u>two</u> and three and <u>four</u> and ... Or in the case of a double beat: One-y-an' a <u>two</u>-y-an' a three-y an' a <u>four</u>-an' a ... Or maybe it's a shuffle beat, using dotted eighth and sixteenth notes: a one, a <u>two,</u> a three, a <u>four,</u> a ... It also shows us where the syncopation is, if any. All of these can be written down. But now we're getting into the more subtle gradations—*groove* and *feel*.

- A *groove* is as real a musical value as any of the others, it's just harder to define because there aren't any standard musical notations for it. A rhythm pattern can be played in several ways: loose and laid-back, or tight and driving; buoyant and on the beat, or spongy and unsettled. "Loose and laid-back" is not necessarily an indication of ineptitude on the part of the players. Some songs sound best that way. "Spongy and unsettled" is another matter. It usually means that some of the players need to "tighten up and relax." One player in a rhythm section needs to be recognized as the captain of the groove, whether it's the leader or the drummer. If every player is a law unto himself, what you have is anarchy, or "spongy and unsettled." But if everybody locks into the groove laid down by the captain of the groove, it feels good.

One mistake some eager but unseasoned musicians make is to confuse speed with groove. We knew one praise band who would constantly try to whip up their audience into a state of excitement. Every song was a headlong rush, accompanied by loud exhortations to praise the Lord with everything in us. The worship leader would shout, "Let's give 110% to the Lord!" It was that extra ten percent that caused the trouble. Everyone felt rushed, pushed, manipulated, driven. Buddy Owens calls it "worship with a gun to your head." From a musical standpoint, what was missing was *groove*. In some cases the *tempo*, or *speed*, might have been right, but it felt nervous and frenzied. If they had just settled back a little and found the groove, their music could have been effective, because they were talented musicians.

In our School of Music Ministries International worship workshops, where the three of us taught together, our band used to demonstrate this principle by stringing together eight bars each of three well known up-tempo praise choruses, all done loudly at mindless breakneck speed, then segueing right into "Roll Out the Barrel (and we'll have a barrel of fun.)" The audience would break out in surprised laughter. Then we would break

> If you're a worship leader, ask yourself: Am I a shepherd or a cowboy? A shepherd leads his flock, a cowboy drives his herd. Is this a worship service or a pep rally? Am I facilitating the people into worship, or am I hyping them? You can whip up a crowd's emotions, but you can't whip up the Holy Spirit. As Michael Harriton said, "A good worship leader creates a draft."

it off and Jimmy would say, "What's wrong with that picture? ... We might as well do that—it's all in the same spirit. It's all hype." Then we would demonstrate each of those three choruses with its own proper tempo and groove, in carefully worked out head arrangements, bringing out the *feeling of the message*. The audience got the point.

- *Feel.* Now we come to the subtlest one of all. Whatever skills you develop as a player or singer, develop *feel*. Playing the right notes isn't enough. **Feel is paramount. Feel is indefinable. Feel is about nuances and subtleties and inflections that can't be written down on paper.** And it comes only with such long hours of practice that the player becomes one with the instrument, and the instrument

Jimmy and Carol

Jimmy and Carol were recording at Capitol Studios and during a break, happened to walk by Studio B, where some rockers were overdubbing their rhythm tracks. After a playback, one of them asked another, "Hey, man, how did that feel?" "It felt great!" his friend answered ... "Sounded terrible, but it felt great!"

Find your groove and go with it.

becomes an extension of the player's thoughts. Feel becomes instinctive, and it defines the difference between an ordinary performer and an artist. As Jeff Crabtree has said, "Nuance is the highest level of technique."

The Cardinal Rule in Arranging and Performance

We realize that in crossing the line from rhythm patterns, which can be written down, to groove and feel, which can't, we've sidestepped a little beyond the scope of this book and are now talking about performing. But since most of our readers are probably also performers, let's expand on it just a little.

Let's apply the Cardinal Rule to arranging and performance as well as to songwriting. The instrumentation, tessitura, tempo, volume, dynamics, tone colors, gestures, facial expressions, instrumental "licks"—all the elements together can support the message, or any one of them inappropriately used can distract from it.

- **Improvised licks can add a lot to a song, but they must agree with and support the message.** For this reason, we believe it's important for the improvising musicians to know what the lyrics are saying, or at least know the feeling they convey. Playing licks just to show off the coolness or cleverness of your playing is fine in instrumental jazz, but in a worship song, (or any song with a message), it's like standing behind the singers and sticking out your tongue and waggling your fingers in your ears. Now you've become a distraction to worship. But properly done, the fills can dialogue with the singer and say "Amen" to the message and help bring it to life.

- And while we're discussing performance, what about **instrumental solos**? How important are they? Instrumental color can provide a refreshing change, so when the voices come back in, it's a fresh sound and the ear is ready for it again. Appropriate instrumental interludes also provide time to meditate on the message. In the Psalms we often encounter the word "Selah." It denotes an instrumental interlude and means "Pause, and calmly think of that." We have seen genuinely anointed instrumental soloists "prophesy" on their instruments and lead a congregation into greater heights of worship. (Guitarist Phil Keaggy is a master at this.) The scripture doesn't say that David sang for Saul, it says he played, and the evil spirit departed. (1 Samuel 16:23)

Intros, Figures, Fills and Endings

How important are introductions, figures, fills and endings and how much attention should the songwriter give to them? Some of these considerations are left entirely up to the arranger, but some songwriters like to present their songs as complete compositions.

- **A good introduction should set up the song: create an ambiance— establish the mood and the feel—and lead straight into the vocal.** There's no set rule as to how long an intro should be. Some consist merely of an arpeggio, while others sound like the first movement of a symphony. But unless the introduction is powerfully exciting in itself, it shouldn't be long.

- Some songs have **"figures"** or countermelodies written into them that appear in every arrangement you hear. A figure is a running thread that recurs throughout the song and gives it a sense of unity and cohesion. Whether it was created by the songwriter or the arranger of the recording or was perhaps improvised by one of the sidemen, it has become the song's "signature lick," an integral part of the song's structure.

- Lyrics don't have to fill up all of every line. In some styles, especially those that use improvising instruments, as in jazz or blues, it's a good idea to use the first half of each four-bar phrase for lyrics, and leave holes, or **"leave some air" for instrumental** *fills*. This makes a refreshing interplay, or conversation, between the voice and the instruments.

- It's possible to become a successful songwriter while offering no more than words, melody and chord symbols, but the more control you have over these other components of your song, the more satisfied you'll be.

- **There are several ways to end a song.**

   1. **A fade.** In some genres it's popular not to end at all but to fade, to give the impression that the participants were last seen boogying off into the sunset. On rhythm section charts for recording we usually notate this "Vamp till fade." (Vamp simply means to continue to improvise on a short repeated chord progression.) But this can be awkward in live performances; "Vamp till fall apart" is usually the impression the audience gets. It's better to bring a live rendition to some sort of satisfying conclusion, such as:

   2. **An extended ending** (stretching out the last few chords or notes)

3. **A delayed ending** (bringing in unexpected chord and melody changes that necessitate repeating the last line) One often used device is a walk-down to the vi minor chord, or simply replacing the final tonic chord with a vi minor, thus indicating to the singers that you are repeating the last line once or twice.

4. **A tag ending or coda** (additional material added on the end)

5. **A "Paramount Ending"** (building to a last-long-loud-high-note)

6. **Just slowing down and coasting to a stop**

7. **An out-tro.** In an especially gentle song that doesn't build to great heights, it's sometimes a good idea to return to the feeling of the intro so that the listener, who has been riding along with us, "gets off where he got on."

8. **A "payoff" ending.** This may be a form of a delayed or extended ending, but with a twist. This happens when the song is building toward a "payoff" last line. You know it's coming… you're waiting for it… but the tension is heightened by building, delaying, extending, perhaps pausing, to set up the "payoff" line. For instance, look at "If My People Will Pray," on page 129. The last line is what everything else in the scripture verse has been leading up to: the culmination, the fulfilment of the promise. So we delay the gratification by repeating "I will forgive their sin" three times, each louder and higher than before, then adding two extra bars and pausing, before delivering, with quiet intensity, the "payoff" line, "and heal their land."

9. **An unfinished ending.** It can also be refreshing on occasion, especially in a quiet mood song, to end on a sustained IV or V or some other "unfinished" chord and let it drift away.

145

In a song for congregational singing, it's best not to put any surprises in the ending, since they can lead to awkward moments of confusion that disturb the flow of worship. **Give thought to how you want your song to end. It leaves a lasting impression.**

Think Syncopation

Syncopation is not something that came in with the jazz age. Martin Luther's original version of "A Mighty Fortress," written in the 16th Century, was heavily syncopated, but as is often the case with church music, by the time it became immortalized it had all the corners squared off.

To syncopate means to modify a rhythm by shifting the accent to a weak beat of the measure, or often to a weak half-beat. We hear it and do it so much that we give it little thought. Syncopation makes the melody "punch" or "float" against the beat instead of marching or plodding on the beat. Syncopation adds rhythmic impetus, but that isn't its only function. It can also help to make stressed and unstressed syllables more closely approximate normal speech patterns. We call it *"singing conversationally."*

Let's look at Carol's worship song, "Wonderful Are Your Works." (Yes, we know it has backward lyrics, but it's quoting a scripture.)

Notice how the syncopation makes the lyric lines flow in normal speech patterns: "Wonderful are Your works, O God! Marvelous are Your ways!" etc.

Sing also the verses of Martin Smith's "I Could Sing of Your Love Forever." "Over the mountains and the sea, Your river runs with love for me," etc. Notice how the words roll off your tongue, almost as if you were not singing at all, but just having a prayerful conversation with the Lord:

You don't use syncopation just to sound cool. When lyrics are involved, the words determine where the punches fall.

Wonderful Are Your Works

Carol Owens

Rhythmic and Dynamic Variety

Going through any song four or five times with no changes of voicing, volume, rhythm pattern, instrumental lines, groove or dynamics is a sure way to bring your congregation crashing down out of the heavenlies.

> The average worship song can be sung once through in less than a minute. If you're trying to fill four or five minutes with that song, the arrangement is very important.

Even in up tempo rhythm, we feel the need of **variety within the unity**. We know it's popular, especially in dance music, to just set up a groove and keep pounding away loudly at it, often without volume changes, all the way through the fade. Maybe that's okay for ear candy. But *dynamics*, the variation in volume, intensity and expression, is the part that often gets forgotten in today's pop music, and the lack of dynamics creates monotony. Without changing the tempo (the speed), what if we **change the *rhythm pattern*** at a suitable place? where the whole texture lightens up for a section, then crescendos back into the original groove?

Look again at the example of "Wonderful are Your Works." The chorus has a driving feeling, with the accents pulsing on every beat: 1 & 2 & 3 & 4 & / 1 & 2 & 3 & 4 &. But at the bridge it lightens up a little and the pattern changes to 1 & 2 & 3 *& 4 &* / 1 & 2 & 3 *& 4 &.* This is called "half time" feel. When we kick back into the next chorus, not only have we *not weakened* the song, but we've avoided monotony and made the pulse feel even stronger for having been given a brief rest.

The *countermelody* can be introduced after the first bridge to increase the variety.

ꝫꝫꝫꝫꝫ

Everything is His,
and all things are from Him,
through Him and to Him. We have
nothing that He has not allowed us to have.
Nothing, in fact, that He hasn't poured out on us.
He is the Great Giver, the Great Provider; Jehovah Jireh.
All He asks is the acknowledgement of grateful hearts.
We need jubilant songs of praise
for that unending generosity.

ꝫꝫꝫꝫꝫ

For another example, listen carefully to Paul's recorded arrangement of "Open the Eyes of My Heart." It takes us on a journey. The verse starts off simply, then builds up to the chorus. Its repeated "Holy holy holy" leads us into awed, meditative worship. As it ends, we feel we've been on a journey and we've been lifted into worship.

Listen to the recording of "Here I Am to Worship," by Tim Hughes. Do you see some of the same qualities? It uses repetition of melody lines, of lyrics, of sections. It uses parallelism, anaphora, (Here I am/here I am; altogether/altogether.) It uses contrast (light/darkness). It establishes a quiet worship atmosphere by using a range of only five notes.

Here again is that journey. Sometimes it takes us beside quiet streams, accompanied only by rhythm guitar, (an intimate, closely held body instrument,) then adds other instruments as it builds to climb hills. Sometimes it inserts an extra bar to let us stop and meditate. As it increases in intensity the vocalists add succeeding inversions above the melody, then the lead worshiper improvises worship lines against this texture. As we reach the highest hilltop, we pause to take in the view (Selah), with an extra measure, a hanging chord and suspended rhythm. This heightens the anticipation of that beautiful, worshipful melody on the chorus as we descend back into the quiet peaceful valley. At the end, it diminishes, has a few bars of free worship, then leaves us drifting away on a IV chord. Well done. So simple, so worshipful, so pure, so quickly learnable, so effective.

But don't let its simplicity fool you. A lot of talent and craftsmanship went into that simple song. How can a song this repetitive, with this small range, be kept alive through over four and a half minutes of repetition? One reason is the constantly changing colors of the *arrangement* that keep it alive through its many iterations.

Rehearse Rehearse Rehearse

When we hear people complain about their church worship team singing simple choruses over and over and over until they don't want to hear them again, it's usually because the team hasn't devoted the time it takes to work out appropriate arrangements on their songs. If they just pass out chord charts and let everyone strum or bang away mindlessly on the chord changes, with no thought of listening to each other, or leaving and filling holes, or playing sensitively with dynamics, is it any wonder the congregation wants to be excused? **Do you see why it takes so much dedication and rehearsal time to be a part of a good worship team?**

The Importance of Style

In this rhythm-driven age, it's a good idea to pay a lot of attention to the musical *style* of your song. Even with great melody and lyrics, your song will have a much better chance of succeeding if it's in a recognizable, authentic, contemporary style with a good rhythm pattern and groove. This has to do partly with the fact that a song is a vehicle for emotional expression. A good popular style is comfortable, familiar and conducive to the expression of feelings. Many a good song has been written starting with a good rhythm pattern. Lots of today's music, including many modern worship songs, incorporates the use of drum machines in its creation. These modern tools inspire the songwriter with subtle rhythmic influences he might not have thought of. Even if the melody flows smoothly in long tones, a bouyant underlying beat can help keep the song alive.

Know the Styles

"Worship Song" is not a style. Worship songs come in many styles. Some churches still worship with pipe organs and hymns. Others use a contemporary guitar-driven style. In yet other churches they may have flavors of country, Southern gospel, Black gospel, blues, jazz, salsa, reggae or other ethnic or "world music" styles. Some mix them all up together.

Each of these styles has characteristics that make it what it is and distinguish it from others. Learn what these characteristics are, and, although hybrid styles do evolve through cross-pollenation, don't mix them without understanding what you're doing. If you put one of these characteristics into a style where it doesn't belong, it may produce a jarring effect that damages the song's authenticity and your credibility. For instance, if you put a major 7th chord, beautiful as it is, in a *traditional* country song, you may get some winces from the purists. But this chord, at home in jazz (but *never* in the blues,) has become acceptable in *pop*-country, now almost synonymous with what was once simply called "pop."

> ### Jazz?
> A fine jazz chord suddenly appearing in the midst of relatively unsophisticated harmony can seem like a tuxedo at a picnic.

As a writer, and especially if you're an arranger or rhythm player, make it your business to become versatile in many styles. You don't have to go to school to do this—just study recordings. Each player should know what his instrument is expected to do in a particular style. In a rehearsal or recording session, if you just hand out chord charts without identifying the style you want, much time can be lost by muddling around trying to figure out what each player is supposed to do, and you may never hit on an authentic style. If you can identify the style by name, the head arrangement will begin to mesh quickly.

APPLICATION:

Spend some time over the next few weeks immersing yourself in various styles of music. Spend a few days listening to nothing except one particular style. Analyze the style by asking yourself a few questions:

1. What kind of chords are they using—triads or sophisticated harmonies?

2. What kind of instrumentation are they using?

3. Are the melodies reaching and soaring, or punchy and tight?

4. What is unique about the feel and mood of this particular style?

Write down your observations and try writing a song incorporating some of these characteristics that you've observed.

• •

Jimmy and Carol
The Philippine Revolution

While they were teaching in the Philippines, Jimmy and Carol met Cardinal Sin, the head of the Catholic Church there. When he was told that they had written *If My People,* he greeted them with surprising warmth. He was suddenly called away, but his secretary explained the cardinal's enthusiasm. He said, "Did you know that your song, 'If My People Will Pray,' was the theme song of our revolution?" The Owenses were astonished.

Earlier, President Marcos's wife, Imelda, a patron of the arts, had asked Pat Boone and the Owenses to put on *If My People* in Luneta Park. Dates were set. Then suddenly it was called off. Because of a Muslim uprising in a south island, Marcos cancelled all Christian appearances.

Shortly after that, the people rose up against the corrupt Marcos regime. Tens of thousands rallied in the streets. During the standoff the people took over a government radio station, and the Jesuits played Jimmy's anthem "If My People Will Pray" around the clock. People sang it at the barricades. The army, instead of firing on the crowds, laid down their arms, and the regime was overthrown, without bloodshed.

After a free election, the new president, Corazon Aquino, held a huge rally in the same park, presenting much of the music and all the major prayers from *If My People.* Jimmy and Carol were thrilled to see a video of the event, as the new president led the crowd in shouting, "Jesus Christ is Lord of the Philippines, and of all nations!"

CHAPTER 7
WORDS AND MUSIC, HAPPY TOGETHER

Matching Words to Melodies

No matter how wonderful a melody may be, if it doesn't match the feeling of the words consistently, it fails to support the message. The ideal we're striving for is to make every melody line, every voicing and chord progression, every rhythm pattern, every choice of words appropriate to the feeling of the message; to create the "Perfect Wedding" of words and music that makes the message come alive. When all the elements are working together, each doing what it's supposed to do, the song has life and warmth and emotion. We don't just hear it, we experience it.

As an excellent example of matching words to melody, let's examine Bob Fitts's beautiful worship song, "Blessed Be the Lord God Almighty."

Blessed Be the Lord God Almighty

The melody starts reverently in the mid-range so it has somewhere to build.

- Notice the end of the first line, *"how we love you."* On *"love you"* the melody has the feeling of bowing down. (What if he had said "how we praise you"? It would work, but "love you" has a softer sound and fits better here.)

- The next line starts high, on the octave, to match the words, "we *lift* your name..." By the end of the line, *"in all the earth,"* the melody line has again descended and bowed down.

- Line 3 is an approximate repeat of the melody of line 1, and line 4 *climbs* with the words "*your mighty works,*" ending back up on the octave.

- The chorus starts on the 5th, or dominant, climbs briefly stepwise before dropping back to the 5th, then leaping up four steps to the octave: "*Blessed be the Lord...*" This interval, 5th to octave, is one of the strongest of all musical intervals, and it places "*Lord*" on the sustained high note on the downbeat of the chorus. This is the hook line, and it has a built-in cry. This hook line, built-in cry and all, is repeated two lines later.

- The last dramatic statement, "*who reigns forever more*" is all high and ends on the octave, diminishes in volume and returns to the verse to start the worship cycle over again.

- The whole chorus of this song soars and draws our hearts and hands up. This song is one of the purest examples of *prosody* (the matching of words to music) we know of. It's the Cardinal Rule in action.

HOW THE SONG WAS BORN
Bob Fitts: Blessed Be the Lord God Almighty

Bob says that in a time of discouragement he picked up his guitar and wrote "Blessed Be the Lord God Almighty" in five or ten minutes. Worship teams from his Youth With a Mission School of Worship in Hawaii took it all over the world. While he was in the stands at the Olympics in Seoul, Korea, he was stunned when thousands began singing his song in Korean. He recalls, "It was too much for me. I just started crying!"

Bob says, "Sing something brand new out of your passion for Jesus. When Jesus is our life, our everything, our songs are believable and authentic. The greatest challenge: getting the song out of your mouth. My wife, Kathy, taught me a lesson about praise while groaning for joy over a piece of warm boysenberry pie. I finally had to ask her to keep quiet or share. She opted for 'keep quiet,' (go figure.) Later she said, 'Wow Bob, you know, after I kept quiet, it just didn't taste as good.' It's like worship and praise: If it just sits in our hearts, it doesn't taste as good. We need to get it out of our souls and bring a new song to birth. Once you've done that, leave the results to God. Keith Green said it so well, 'You just do your best, pray that it's blessed, and He'll take care of the rest.' You and I need to be faithful to sing our songs out, and trust then that God will appoint, anoint and grant favor where it's needed."

Now let's look at a great masterpiece of melody, this one over four hundred years older.

A Mighty Fortress Is Our God

Martin Luther

This hymn starts with a descending line, with great grandeur to match its grand subject. Ringing prime notes on the octave, like great bells, lift our eyes to the imagery of God as a towering fortress. The notes on "a bulwark never failing" march downhill, treading their message of triumph into bedrock certainty on the root of the key. Line two is an exact copy of line one, repeating the triumphal process, after which the melody develops in other directions but ends exactly as lines one and two end; it returns to familiar ground, offering a sense of finality.

The most obvious thing these two worship songs, so different from each other, have in common is their adherence to the Cardinal Rule: all the elements work together to make the message come to life.

Ups and Downs

If the visual imagery of a lyric has a sense of vertical dimension, it's a good idea, though not a hard and fast rule, for the melody to go in the same direction. Look again at Paul's "Revival Fire Fall." Do you see the principle, right there in the first falling melody line?

Look also at "Like a rose trampled on the ground, You took the fall." What if he had decided to write an ascending melody on those words? There's no law against it, but doesn't the descending line match the thought better?

However, don't drive yourself crazy with this. Trying to match every up and down and punch and accent between a lyric and its music is called "Mickey Mousing," a term derived from the work of early cartoon scorers. But do be aware of the principle.

APPLICATION:

So far in this chapter we've seen several examples of the imagery of lines. Here's a little exercise you might try—imagine yourself in these various physical postures, then create a line of melody that matches each posture:

- Reaching out to help someone

- Embracing someone

- Bowing down in worship

- Reaching up in worship

- Taking a stand against evil

- Standing tall but serene, with head held high

- Strutting with pride

- Celebrating a great victory

- Rocking a baby, or being rocked in the Lord's arms

Here's a hint on the last one—remember Kurt Kaiser's beautiful chorus, "Oh How He Loves You and Me"? Right at the end it repeats the melody line twice before ending. This melodic repetition, coupled with the repetition of the chords, in 3/4 time—doesn't that make you feel as though you're being rocked like a baby in loving arms? There is no more universal longing than that. That's what made that song the enormous hit it was in the church all over the world.

You might want to think of some other postures and set them to melody.

Our Cardinal Rule can be summed up in one key word: *Appropriateness*

By *appropriateness* we mean good taste and common sense, not just spirituality. We don't want to set the Lord's Prayer or any other reverent expression of worship to a slick, frivolous dance beat. Some styles were never intended to carry the weight of message—they're simply dance music. Of course there's a place for joyful expressions of praise in say, a happy reggae beat. The Bible tells us to dance before the Lord. David did it, with all his might, to wild and exuberant music. Just be careful that your music consistently fits your message. You don't want to realize suddenly that you've turned a corner into solemn words of worship and find yourself boogying into the Throne Room, to the amazement of all the worshiping seraphim and saints. Oops!

Another form of inappropriateness is *overfamiliarity with the Lord,* as in two imaginative titles submitted to a publisher we knew—"Curly Hair, Eyes of Blue—That's My Jesus," and "Holding Hands With Jesus on the Beach at Waikiki." Perhaps the most insensitive kind of all is "Jesus died on Calvaree, Shed his blood to set me free" snap snap groove groove grin grin— a careless disregard for the gravity, pathos and meaning of the passion. Although there is a wealth of subject matter within our Christian experience to celebrate in "fun" music, Jesus' agony on the cross is not a subject of fun for any thinking person.

ვვვვ

Up on
the mountain,
Jesus was transfigured
in front of Peter, James and John.
In the middle of this transcendent spiritual
revelation unequalled in all human history, Peter
said the wrong thing again. But Jesus didn't rebuke him.
He saw a good man overawed by the Glory. He saw a heart filled
with worship and the fear of the Lord. And there is the
beginning of wisdom. Oh, Father, fill me, too, with
that wonderful awe that ignites and burns
with the love of God and brings
me to my knees.

ვვვვ

Setting Scripture to Music

Many beginning writers try to start by writing scripture songs. That way, they think they won't have to worry too much about the lyrics. But these are some of the hardest songs to write well. First, let's list **some common mistakes** and see if we can give some constructive help:

1. **Trying to cram all the exact words of scripture** into too few beats, putting acCENTS on the wrong sylLAbles. Carol says, "Like a lady trying to squeeze into a girdle, something is usually left hanging over in the wrong place."

2. **Starting a song with the word "for" or "therefore."** Both these words refer back to something previous, and if your song starts there and doesn't refer back to anything, you raise questions that don't get answered.

3. **Mixing King James English with modern English.** Once you've addressed the Lord as "You," don't switch the form of address to "Thee" to make a rhyme.

- On the positive side, keep several Bible translations handy so you can find various wordings of verses. Some are more lyrical than others and may fit your meter better. If none of them works, make your own paraphrase. Yes, it's perfectly all right to do this. After all, you're not claiming your version is scripture—only lyrics based on scripture.

- But be careful. **Don't attempt a paraphrase on the strength of one translation.** Unless you know Biblical Hebrew or Greek, stay very close to the consensus of several translations. The Amplified Bible can give you added insight into shades of meaning, and a thesaurus may help, too. If any interpretation of doctrine is involved, it's a good idea to have your lyrics checked by someone who knows theology. A subtle shade of meaning

Jimmy and Carol

In their early days of writing musicals, the Owenses had to sit and go over every song and script with a panel assembled by their publisher, which included a pastor/theologian. Jimmy and Carol called it The Inquisition, but they were grateful for it. Better to fix a problem before it's published than to find it afterward.

might imply doctrinal error that could raise red flags in at least some parts of the church.

- If you really want to set a scripture verse to music verbatim (perhaps as an aid to Bible memorization), here's a starting place: In some translations, the translators have rendered the Psalms and a few other poetic passages into at least a type of free verse. They don't rhyme, but by stretching words and syllables over several notes you might establish some meter with them, especially if you repeat some phrases.

- **Consider the *sounds* of the words in your scripture passage.** Don't expect to find much rhyme; but look for poetic qualities such as assonance, consonance, alliteration, etc. A verse such as "He walks on the wings of the wind" (Psalm 104:3) might almost set itself to music.

Ed Kerr and Paul were assigned to write a scripture memory song for a passage in Psalm 103, from the NIV Bible. Their first thought was, "Nothing rhymes. This is going to be impossible." But as they carefully read the scriptures out loud and began singing the words with random melodies, they were pleasantly surprised to find their mouths delighting in all the yummy alliteration, assonance and inner rhymes that were coming out. Say it aloud to yourself, and notice all the devices there:

Bless the Lord, O my soul
(Two O's and two el's in that line)
And forget not all His benefits.
(Alliteration: three tees)
Who forgives all your sins and heals all your diseases.
(Assonance: two short i's and two ee's. And listen to the six zee sounds. There are

seven esses, all but one pronounced as zees.)
Who redeems your life from the pit
(Nothing much in that line)
and crowns you with love and compassion.
(Two hard cees and two uh sounds)
He satisfies your desires with good things
(Two long i's and three zees)
So that your youth is renewed like the eagle's.
(Isn't that lovely?)

You may not notice all that just by looking at a passage, but if you read it aloud and sing it out, you may discover some real poetic beauty in the scriptures.

•**Look for obvious rhythm patterns in the passage.** Sometimes the first phrase will establish a rhythm pattern you can develop. The rhythm of "You Shall Be Holy," from *If My People* ... was suggested by the inner rhyme *be* and *Me:*

You shall be
Holy unto Me
For I, the Lord, am holy.

Jon Mohr's touching scripture song, "He Who Began a Good Work in You" develops in the same way, emphasizing the alliteration between "He" and "who" and placing "who" and "you" in rhyming spots:

He   who
Began a good work in you

Or maybe you can make the text fit the meter by **stretching some syllables over two or more beats or notes,** (called *melisma)* as in "Gloria In Excelsis Deo."

- A time-honored way of making a scripture passage lyrical is to use **the anthem form**. A song may say, "The cows are in the corn," while an anthem says, "The cows, the cows, the cows, are in the corn, the corn, the corn." Rewind to page 129 and read the lyrics to Jimmy's "If My People will Pray." The whole scripture passage is there, its meaning is intact, but the words have been converted from prose to lyrics.

Translating

If you're translating songs from one language to another, don't sacrifice lyricism. In your diligence to provide a faithful translation, you won't be doing the original lyricist any favors by making his ideas sound awkward and stilted. A phrase that is imaginative and has a lovely cadence in Italian, for instance, may be prosaic and pedestrian in a too literal English translation. The best way to respect the writer's intentions is to write a lyric in the new language that is true to the ideas and message of the original but is a lyric in its own right. This may involve shifting the position of some of the phrases for grammatical or rhyming considerations, although you should be careful to keep the main hook lines, especially title lines, in their original positions.

Some languages require more words or syllables to say something than others do. The more words a language has in common usage, the fewer words may be needed to express a thought precisely. For instance, if you have a choice of several verbs, one of which speaks with great nuance and precision, you may not need an adverb to intensify it.

> English is such a great language for lyric writing! It has three times as many words as any western European language, often giving us the luxury of choosing between several words, each with a subtly different shade of color and meaning.

You may think, "But I only speak one language, so this doesn't apply to me." But you might be involved in the translation process even if you don't speak the original language. Here's how: Translating may sometimes be done by a team consisting of a translator and a lyricist. The translator knows both languages well and can make a more or less literal translation, but may have no gift at all as a lyricist. In this case the translator shouldn't be concerned about economy of words. On the contrary, he or she might add in extra words that help to clarify and bring out all the subleties and shades of meaning in the original. He might want to adapt the grammatical form, or syntax, to the new language, but even then the words may not flow and almost certainly won't rhyme. But now the lyricist steps in and expresses the feelings and meanings of the message in lyrical language. The translator can then check the lyricist's work for accuracy. **Remember, in any language, lyrics are words that sing.**

• •

Jimmy and Carol
The Witness

After the intercessory groundwork laid by *Come Together* and *If My People,* it was time for evangelization. The Owenses wrote *The Witness*, Jesus' story as told by Peter. This musical was put on in many nations, and is still being done. It has run all summer every year since 1980 at an ampitheatre in Hot Springs, Arkansas, and has been promoted by the Chamber of Commerce as their Passion Play. A large church in North Carolina has presented *The Witness* multiple times every Easter since 1979, where many hundreds have come to Christ through its ministry.

CHAPTER 8
HOW TO STIMULATE CREATIVITY

Twelve Keys to Unlock Writer's Block

We all have times when music flows freely. And we all have times when "the heavens are as brass" and we just can't seem to break through spiritually. Or maybe we're in a rut where all our songs are beginning to sound alike, at least to other people. How do we get the juices flowing again? It depends on what's causing the blockage. If it's because we're spiritually dry and don't have anything fresh to say, the answer is obvious—we need a fresh drink of Living Water. But if we're just musically dry, maybe we need to listen to some music. Especially when we try to write in an unaccustomed style, we need to soak ourselves in that particular stream for awhile. We don't want to copy other people's ideas; we just want to prime our pumps and refresh our memory of the characteristics of the genre.

The Apostle Paul wrote to Timothy, "Stir up the gift that is within you." He was referring to a spiritual gift, but the same principle applies to the musical gift. Warm-up exercises stir athletes and singers to top performance, and they work for songwriters too. **Try some of these ideas to get the creative flow started:**

1. *Chord changes.* Find a collection of good songs and look for unusual chord changes. These may spark fresh melodic ideas that might not have occurred to you otherwise. The chord change you started with may not appear in the final version of your song—but it's served as a jump start when your battery was low.

2. *Rhythm patterns.* Select a groove and start singing some lyric ideas over it. New riffs may spark new melodies. Lots of today's music, including many modern worship songs, incorporate the use of drum machines in their creation. These modern tools can inspire you with subtle rhythmic influences you might not have thought of.

3. *Another key.* If you've fallen into the habit of looking for melodies in keys like C, D or Eb, where the tonic lies near the bottom of the staff, try playing around in F, G or Ab, which put the tonic closer to the middle of the range. This will force you away from melodies that keep ending up high or low. You may get an entirely different feeling from one of these keys.

Or try experimenting in keys you don't normally play in because they're too difficult. Work at them until they become easier. This will not only make you a more complete musician, it may even suggest new melodies to you by keeping your fingers from falling where the ideas may be all fished out. Maybe you need to try some different fishing holes for a change.

One of Paul's favorite ways to write is to walk around the room and begin singing out scripture passages and lines from his journal or "singing his prayers." Paul writes 90% of his songs without an instrument. "It takes me places I would never go with an acoustic guitar."

4. **Writing A Cappella.** Try searching for a melody without using an instrument. The problem is that our fingers tend to develop habits of their own, and when we let them do the walking they tend to walk to the same old places over and over. When we take them out of the process, we may find ourselves freed up to head in some new directions. We can harmonize our melody later.

5. *Another mode.* How long has it been since you've fished around in a minor key? Don't forget about them; they can take you to a whole new place.

6. *Experimenting with scale tones.* Play them over and see what ideas come. For example, start your melody on the 3rd degree of the scale. Then try starting on the 6th degree, or the 2nd.

7. *Matching chords to lyrics.* Look closely at your words—what is the *overall feel* of your message? What kinds of chords does it need? Try putting appropriate chords under certain key words or phrases, such as:

   • Ringing triads for a triumphant line

   • An add 9 or 6-9 for a lush, beautiful scene

   • A major 7th for a peaceful and serene thought

   • A triad with no 3rd (a C5 or a G5 chord) for a Celtic, anthemic quality

   • A iv minor 6 for a nostalgic feeling

   • A ♭vii for a serious statement or a classic rock feel

   • A discordant alternate bass note for an ominous part

See what melodic ideas develop from them. Then work backwards and forwards from there to flesh out your melody.

8. *Detuning your guitar.* Tune your low E string down to a D and experiment with "Dropped D" tuning. Or tune your high E string down a half step and every chord will sound different. E will be Emajor7, etc. It may create a different mood, full of new ideas. Perhaps try using a "cut capo."

9. *Playing along with a recording.* Is this cheating? Of course not, as long as you don't actually steal something. You'd be surprised how many successful writers do this. What you're looking for is a jump start—something to get you into a genre and a feel that have already proven successful. After you've played along for a while, turn off the recording and improvise your own stuff. You may find you've turned a corner and the new material coming out of you now is your own. Something in there may spark the beginning of a song. But when you're through, listen again to the recording to make sure that what you've wound up with really is yours. It's sometimes hard to remember whether what you find yourself singing or playing was your idea or someone else's.

Remember though, in all these attempts—don't create a mechanical melody. Use these devices only as a starting point and let your own creativity take over. When you're experimenting, you may want to turn on a tape recorder and forget about it. If something good comes you've got it. If not, you haven't lost anything.

10. *Take a break.* Relax. If you've been working long and hard on your song and ideas have ceased to flow, you've probably worked your creativity into shutdown mode. Move around and get your mind on something else, something enjoyable that doesn't take too much

thought. A little R and R can literally re-create your ability to think and solve problems. When you come back you may have a breakthrough. Paul likes to go out and mow his lawn when he's stuck.

11. *Sleep on It.* Apparently there really is something to that old adage. There is a stage at the edge of sleep, coming or going, during which our creativity is said to be at its highest. Just before you go to sleep, run over in your mind a song you're working on. When you wake up, check it again and see if anything new has developed.

12. *Pray About It.* Sometimes, even in spite of our best efforts to prime our pumps, we still draw a blank, and if we're up against a deadline, we find ourselves in trouble. That's when we need extra special help from the Source of our creativity. (Of course this doesn't mean, "Wait until all else fails—then pray.")

Jimmy and Carol

Years ago, after midnight on the night before a big recording session with a large orchestra, Carol went into Jimmy's study and saw by the glazed expression in his burned-out eyes that he was in Big Trouble. His pencil sat idle on the score page and his brain had stopped going beep … beep … beep … beep and was now going beeeeeeeeeeeeeeeeeep… She rushed into the bedroom, threw herself down at the bedside and cried out in frustration, "Lord, do you know what it's like when you're trying to create something?!" Then she realized what she had just said, and burst into helpless laughter. But when she went back to check on her poor husband, she found that her blurted prayer had been heard—Jimmy was now hearing such a rush of ideas that he could hardly scribble them all down fast enough.

APPLICATION:

Try some of the Keys to Unlock Writer's Block listed above. Or try them even if you don't have writer's block—just for fun.

Who is like Him
The Lion and the Lamb
Seated on the throne
Mountains bow down
Every ocean roars
To the Lord of Hosts
(Chorus)
Praise Adonai
From the rising of the sun
'Til the end of every day
Praise Adonai
All the nations of the earth
All the angels and the saints
Sing praise

(Praise Adonai, by Paul Baloche)

Twelve Tools to Make Your Job Easier

Here are some tools that can help every songwriter. You can write without any of them, of couse, but they make your task easier:

1. **Rhyming Dictionary.** Rest assured that it is *not* cheating to use a rhyming dictionary to help you find words that rhyme. It will save you a great deal of time and trouble, and there is no virtue in sitting there running over "dog, fog, log, nog, sog, yog and zog" in your head.

2. **Dictionary.** To check your spelling as well as the exact meaning of words.

3. **Thesaurus.** To help you find just the *right* words. *Roget's International Thesaurus* says, "In a dictionary, you start with a word and look for its meaning. In a thesaurus, you start with your idea and find words

172

to express it." For instance, Roget's contains more than one hundred words or phrases used to describe or express worship. Most good word processing programs have spellcheckers and thesauruses (thesauri?) built in, but in our experience, they aren't nearly as extensive as Roget's.

4. **Basic grammar book.** Check it when in doubt. Incorrect grammar is okay if it fits the character you're writing about, as in the gospel favorite, "Can't Nobody Do Me Like Jesus." Otherwise, be careful to avoid basic errors.

5. **Bible Concordance.** To find scripture verses. All you need is a key word to help you find what you need.

6. **Several Bible translations.** Often the wording in one version will fit a melody better than any of the others.

7. **Topical Bible.** A great help is *Nave's Topical Bible,* where you can look up a subject like "God, love of" and find all the scriptures on that theme already listed and written out for you. This is also available as a software program.

8. **Recorder.** To help catch transient ideas before you lose them. One friend woke in the middle of the night, sang into his recorder, then went back to sleep. The next morning he played it back and heard, in his words, "a sepulchral voice singing absolute nonsense." Glenn Hegel tells us, "I used to wake up in the night with a melody or lyric and think, 'I'll remember it.' Wrong. Now I sleep with a recorder next to my bed, so I can record it before I fall back to sleep. It makes for very entertaining listening in the morning. The sound quality is even better when you're trying to sing into a recorder at 3:30am and not wake up your spouse." Paul simply calls his own cell phone and leaves

himself a melodic message. After using and losing various portable recording devices over the years, he finds that a phone never fails to capture a moment of inspiration.

9. **Music paper.** To write down ideas as they occur.

10. **Pocket notebook and pencil.** Jimmy calls his "the visible half of my brain." Have you ever had the experience of getting a song idea and having no place to write it down? Did you keep singing it over and over, afraid if you stopped singing you'd lose it? Of course; it happens to all of us. Most of us don't carry score paper around in our pockets, but a simple 3X5 inch lined pocket pad will serve to catch fleeting tunes before they get away. Here's how. Draw a treble clef over three lines, then quickly draw two lines between them and what have you got? Ta—da! A music staff that's good enough for scribbling until you can copy it on real music manuscript paper. Caution: Do not attempt to write down a song while driving. Pull over.

11. **Song collections.** Play them over, listening for fresh chord changes. Read the lyrics and look for rhymes, alliteration, matching vowel sounds, etc. Look especially for good imperfect rhymes.

12. **Idea files.** Journals and folders to keep thoughts you've jotted down on scraps of paper, envelopes, napkins, post-it notes, etc., things you feel the Lord saying to you. Don't throw anything away. Go through it occasionally and see if song ideas arise.

Let's Get Together and Write a Song

Sometimes you just have to face facts: Let's suppose you've done everything you could. You've listened, analyzed and written and rewritten and rewritten. But no matter how you try, your lyrics still sound like sermons or essays rather than flowing, singing lyrics.

Or let's suppose the lyrics are coming along great, but the tunes are unexciting, unemotional and, well, dull. It could be that melody is not your gift. If you, like most of us, can't do all these things well, don't feel bad— find a collaborator. It's better to be half, or even a third, of a team that really flies than to insist on doing it all yourself and never get off the ground. Each writer brings something different to the table: new ideas, hooks, images, words; new styles or techniques. Pay attention. Soak it up, and you'll not only have a better song, but you'll become a better writer. Remember Solomon's advice, "Two are better than one, because they have a good return for their work. If one falls down, his friend can help him up." (Ecclesiastes 4:9-10a (NIV).

> **Synergism**
> Co-writing has its advantages. It can unlock writer's block, and it's a great way to develop your craft.

But, collaboration is an art, and it's not for the faint hearted. Check your ego at the door. What's needed here are humility and teachableness. (This doesn't mean you never stick to your guns if you think your idea works best, but it's good if you can explain why you think so.) You'll need to be humble enough to accept a new direction or toss a pet idea—(grit your teeth)—if a better one comes along. And remember to save that great idea for later.

When you co-write, you come up against the age-old question: which comes first, melody or lyrics? The answer is—whatever feels *inspired* first. Experiment and find out what works best for you. Some composers don't like to be handed a completed lyric because it squeezes them into a preset metric and rhythmic mold. Some prefer it, asking the lyricist to make minor changes later to fit the tune, if necessary. Some develop words and music together line by line.

Many of the songs Paul wrote with Ed Kerr came this way. Ed would sit at the piano while Paul walked around the church sanctuary, speaking and singing out scriptures, prayers and lines from his journal—worshiping. Ed would listen and put interesting chords under the free form melody lines Paul was creating. At other times Ed would suggest melodic ideas and Paul would find interesting guitar chords to put underneath. A lot of those songs were finished and recorded, then recorded by many others. Looking back at them, Paul feels that those melodies tended to be more original than some of his others.

Paul and Ed were equipped with **the co-writer's most important tools: diplomacy, good manners, compassion ... and thick skin.** They understand that you can be stubborn about making changes and have a second-rate song, or you can *be objective* (easier said than done) and have a better song. This is a team effort and the goal is *a strong song*.

Some people find this hard to do. We know of one married couple who wrote one song together—a *great* song. One of them continued through the years to write many great songs, but they never wrote together again. When asked why, their answer is, "We decided to stay married."

Jimmy and Carol started writing together almost by accident. Jimmy was writing a song, got hung up on the lyrics, and asked Carol for help. So they went to work and discovered they enjoyed writing together. It wasn't long before songwriting (especially musicals) became their major and arranging became Jimmy's minor. Who writes which? They both do both, Jimmy more music and Carol more lyrics. They agree that neither of them could have done most of the things they've done without the other.

Paul's wife Rita has written many modern church standards, including "I Will Celebrate," "Rock of Ages" and "But For Your Grace." Rarely have they sat down to write a song together, but they freely critique each other's material with the goal of helping the other person finish strong.

Last, but first of all: Never forget an opening time of prayer—getting your spirits straight and happy; calling for inspiration from the Holy Spirit. Worship together. This is fundamental to a great collaboration.

• •

Paul

Ed Kerr and I used to meet at our church early in the morning where we shared an office. Ed was a classical piano player with a master's degree in performance. I was an electric guitar player who had been in and out of rock bands since high school. We respected each other's differences and tried to stay open minded when the other guy brought an idea to the table. We would make some coffee, pray, open our Bibles, and begin singing out either some psalms or some of our journal ideas. Sometimes this would go nowhere but it was a way of getting some momentum. Conquering inertia is half the battle. Over a period of three years we wrote and demoed over 200 songs. We made a commitment to writing. We believed that if we just "showed up", eventually we would get better. We wrote a lot of bad songs. But we wrote a few good ones in the process, and perhaps more importantly, we learned a lot by having our songs rejected over and over again and paying attention to "what wasn't working".

Over the years I 've had the opportunity to co-write with lots of other writers. Some of the best experiences came with guys like Gary Sadler, Lenny LeBlanc and Don Moen, who always showed up with a handful of ideas and a willingness to let those ideas be changed and rearranged. Sometimes a writer would bring the lyrics and someone else would work on the music. Claire Cloninger used to fax or email me a lyric with a note that said "This one sounds like you". It was always an exciting challenge to marry her lyric to some music that supported the message.

177

To date, Claire has over 400 songs being tracked by CCLI. Wow! She is prolific because she decided years ago that she was going to "show up" and write every day, trusting that inspired ideas would fall from heaven through her hands.

Claire Cloninger's Top Ten Tips

1. **Pray before songwriting sessions.** Ask God to fill you, empower you and use your gifts to bring him glory.

2. **Worship as you're writing worship.** The best worship songs don't flow out of a vacuum or out of a distracted and cluttered mind but out of a worshipful heart.

3. **Don't write the whole Bible in every song.** Learn to center around one key idea. Keep a notebook with you at all times. Don't let any stray song ideas get away.

4. **Learn to re-write.** In the Parable of the Talents, the master was only angry with the servant who buried his talent and didn't make the most of it. I believe when we refuse to rewrite our songs until they are the best they can be we are like the servant who buried his talent.

5. **Cultivate Co-writers.** I am totally handicapped (much like a one-legged man) since I write only lyrics. I owe a great debt to the gifted composers who have invited my words to take a ride on their melodies for the last 25 years! But even if you write both words and music you too can benefit by co-writing. I have honed my abilities and deepened in my faith by collaborating. You can too.

6. **Create an office space.** Even if it's only a desk of your own, get all of your songwriting materials together in one place.

7. **Write every day if you can.** If you're a writer, you will write.

8. **Listen to music.** In addition to worship music, listen to some classical, pop, jazz, whatever you enjoy. And be sure to reserve some quiet times to listen for God's still, small voice!

9. **Find two or three close friends who will pray daily for your writing and seek the Lord with you for direction.** Ask them periodically to pray with you in person.

10. **Take advantage of opportunities to grow in your songwriting skills.** Attend seminars. Read books like this one and subscribe to worship magazines.

Free-for-all Songwriting?

> There's no rule that says a collaboration has to be limited to two writers.

Sometimes it's easier to settle differences of opinion when you have three writers rather than only two; two of you can always gang up on the other one. But sometimes even that doesn't work; there's always the chance of a three-way split.

Here's a fun experiment for you: **get several talented people together—** maybe a band or even a class, **and try writing a song together.** Some may be better at lyrics, others at music.

- First, establish some ground rules. You need a warm, nourishing atmosphere for your plants to grow, so Rule One is that anybody can throw in ideas without fear of rejection. Arctic winds chill creative juices.

- Agree on a topic, an idea, then brainstorm together. Begin clustering. Assign one person to write on a board all the concepts that are presented and someone else to play musical ideas as they arise. Ideas spark ideas.

- Set a groove. Develop a chord progression. Find a motif and develop it into a melody. Let words and music grow together simultaneously. Suggest better words, ideas, chords, hooks, keep improving. See where this takes you. Someone (the teacher?) must be the final arbiter, or maybe you can arrive at the finished version democratically. This is lots of fun and sometimes has produced good songs.

You might want to get together with a group of likeminded songwriters about once a month and get opinions of your works-in-progress from one another.

When you're critiquing, be kind. First say what feels good about the song. If you have problems with it, say, " ... but it has a yellow flag (or a red flag)," then point out the problem. If they try to justify and explain it, say "I'm not going to let you get away with that. This is too good a song. Put it back in the greenhouse. Water it some more, worship with it." It's amazing how "iron sharpens iron" and creativity begets creativity.

Building Your Craft

To recap, there are four disciplines for a songwriter:

Listen, Analyze, Write, Rewrite

- *Listen* to many different kinds of music from classical to contemporary. It's wonderful that you want to write worship songs, but if you listen only to worship songs you won't have anything new to bring to the genre. Writers who say, "I never listen to other music because I want to be original," soon become boring. Without fresh influences, their minds reprocess only the old, and all their songs begin to sound alike. Eventually they'll be going round and round in their own little eddy while the rest of the creative river flows past. But as you let your sphere of music appreciation become more elastic, you'll stretch as a writer. Listening supplies your subconscious music machine with new fodder to digest and synthesize.

- *Analyze* great music from many other writers. They teach us and prime our pumps. Don't pattern yourself after any one writer, no matter how great he or she is, or the best you can hope to be is a clone. Let yourself be influenced by all the best, so your own genius can grow out of the same roots as theirs.

When you find a song that stands head and shoulders above others, study it and find out why it works. In March, 2001, the National Endowment for the Arts and the RIAA (the Recording Industry Association of America) jointly named "Over the Rainbow," by Harold Arlen and E.Y. Harburg "the top song of the Twentieth Century." A group of legendary songwriters, including Paul McCartney and Brian Wilson, polled by the British magazine, *Mojo*, named it "one of the three greatest songs ever written." And in June, 2004, the American Movie Institute named it "the number one movie song of all time." What can you learn from it?

What is it about certain songs that makes people square their shoulders and lift their heads? What makes this music different from tunes that make people want to get down and boogie? Or get down and worship? Not, what do you *feel* that's different about them, but what *musical devices* make you feel what you feel? *How* do feel-good songs make us feel good, for instance? *How* do their melodies, chords and rhythms achieve the effects you want your song to have?

You can find out only by listening, analyzing and experimenting. We could go on pointing out different qualities of memorable music, but our purpose is to help launch you on some investigative journeying of your own.

With all our emphasis on analysis, don't worry if you seem to be getting *too* analytical for a while. We heard a preacher describing a golfing buddy who would get so tied up in placing his feet, his fingers, his wrists and his back in the correct position that he couldn't hit the ball in the right direction. Golfers call it *"the paralysis of analysis."* But this is only a transitional stage. If the golfer doesn't learn these things and practice them well, he will probably never be a good golfer. If he hangs in there, the techniques will become second nature to him and his golf game will be better than ever.

This can happen with songwriting as well. That's why we stress: Study the principles of songwriting. Become aware of them in every song you hear. Absorb them into your subconcious so that they become a part of you.

- *Write*, and keep writing. Keep your mental and spiritual songwriting muscles in shape. Don't just talk about writing, or imagine yourself writing, but write, write, write. When you write, just write. Let the ideas flow freely. If you have the principles built into you, they will come out naturally in your writing. They will serve as safeguards, to keep you from writing poor quality stuff.

Write from your heart. Rewrite from your head. They're both important to the process.

- *Rewrite.* This is where the hardest work comes in, but it's at this level that we fashion a work worthy of offering to the Lord, and to the people. Ask yourself, how can I improve these lines that have flowed out of me? *This* is when you get analytical. Pick your work apart mercilessly and make it better.

If music is important to you, learn all you can about it. Serious painters may spend a year in Paris, hanging out at the Louvre, copying the masters. If you want to get better, find someone better than you and learn from him or her. Become a life long student of great songs. Pay attention to the songs that move you. Drag them back to your woodshed and take them apart and analyze them. Ask yourself—what's going on here? As you take time to discover these lyrical, melodic or harmonic jewels, they will become part of your own ever expanding musical palette. The more you know, the better you'll be.

To recap, a successful worship song will be:

1. Scriptural

2. Universal

3. Emotional (a built-in cry)

4. Uplifting

5. Fresh and original

6. Simple (only one idea, or two at most)

7. Built on a strong hook

8. Repetitive

9. Predictable (sequential)

10. In the common range (A) B♭ up to D (E♭)

11. Melodically interesting

12. Harmonically simple but colorful

13. Easy to sing

14. Easy to learn

15. Easy to remember

16. Hard to forget

All the elements will work together to make the feeling of the message come alive.

APPLICATION:

Check some of your songs for these qualities. Where you find your songs lacking, improve them.

How Do I Know When My Song is Really Ready?

Jimmy and Carol had a friend who was a reviewer of songs for a major Christian music company. They sat in his office one day as he shoved some demo tapes around on his desk and sighed. "I get a lot of songs with strong starts—a good four bar hook—then everything falls apart. Can't anybody finish a song anymore?" Another reviewer expressed the same frustration—"A lot of them start off okay, but somehow the train never gets out of the station."

Your song should be self-contained: strong start, strong middle, strong logical finish, no loose ends, no rambling, no confusion as to what this song is about. In our classes we've all three had students who wanted to go into lengthy explanations before presenting their songs. We asked them, as kindly as we could, not to explain the song, just sing it. When you have to explain your song it means you don't feel good about it. You can't follow it around explaining it every time somebody sings it. So make sure it speaks for itself without explanation before you ever release it.

You'll know your song is ready when it's the best you can make it. Don't be an early settler. Polish and repolish your song, hone it and distill it, until you're sure there's nothing more you can add to it and nothing you can take away.

Chris Tomlin

"I usually am never able to finish a song immediately. It's usually best to let your songs have time to develop into something more wonderful than you originally planned. I see so many stubborn writers who don't want any part of the song to be changed. A mature writer knows when a song is finished."

ʒʒʒʒʒ

Be so convinced of the power of your
gift that you dedicate yourself to
the work of excellence.
No negligence.
No second best.
Of course, your song
may not be perfect. In
fact, sometimes it
may not work at
all. That's
all right;
put it aside
and try again.
But even a failure
should always be the best
you can do with <u>that</u> song.

ʒʒʒʒʒ

CHAPTER 9
GETTING YOUR SONGS HEARD

We said earlier that you don't have to be a worship leader to write songs, just a worshiper. But being a worship leader does have its advantages. It gives you a laboratory to try out your new songs, and a platform to have your songs heard. So if you're not a worship leader, you need to have at least some sort of connection with a church music department, or someone you can show your new songs to who might be able to get them used and heard.

It's amazing to see how the Lord sometimes opens doors for His children and engineers us into doing things that we never would have expected.

For instance, Paul was content to be just "the guitar guy," touring with artists and playing in the church worship band. One Sunday his pastor, Albie Pearson, asked him publicly to lead a worship song. He did it reluctantly at first, but it was a beginning. Fourteen years later he's still serving at the same church as a lead worshiper, composer, recording artist and teacher.

Jimmy was a newly converted trumpet player. He volunteered for the church orchestra and was asked to lead the church music department "temporarily." He was there 15 years. He started composing when the church needed songs on special themes.

Carol was singing in the church's services and on its broadcasts. She wrote her first lyrics when Jimmy was stuck and needed help on a song. They became a songwriting team. This led the two of them to recording, touring and teaching.

And by the way, J.S. Bach was the music director at his local church in Leipzig for 25 years.

Breaking and Entering

We've been asked occasionally, "How can I break into Christian music?" The answer to that is, breaking and entering is illegal, but if you diligently prepare yourself to be the best you can be and accept the small opportunities, the Lord may surprise you by breaking down some doors for you and placing you where He wants you.

Of course this doesn't mean you just sit back and wait for something to happen. You need to be involved in music ministry in some way to gain the recognition that leads to open doors. Did you notice the similarity in each of our stories above? All three of us were playing or singing in church when the first small steps began. You saw this in some of the other writers' stories too.

This is a key: **Write for your local church instead of for imagined big projects.** Serve your local congregation. You know them and they know you. If your songs work for them they may work at large.

The Bible says "Put off selfish ambition and striving." We can't emphasize

Matt Redman

A great sign that part of your calling is to songwriting is when those around you recognize and affirm that calling on your life. In an ideal situation it will be a leader in your church who plays this role.

this enough. We've met so many people who are constantly frustrated because they have put God in a box. Instead of faithfully serving their local body and letting God promote in His timing, they

> Be faithful in small things. Be prepared when opportunities come. Let God do the promoting.

are anxiously trying to "make it happen." Get their songs out there, get published, get famous. The highest goal should be to help people fall in love with the Lord.

Mark Altrogge recommends:

"If your song works within a local setting, then send it out to the churches that you're a part of and see if it takes off there." That's what happened to him. "I Stand in Awe" was as great a song on the day he finished it as it is now, but it had to have that first hearing in humble surroundings for God to open up the path for it. It spread until it was picked up by Integrity and recorded on a Bob Fitts album, and from there it went all over the world.

Philippians 2:13 (NIV) says, "It is God who works in you to will and to do what pleases Him." And this is not always a comfortable process. Jimmy reflects that some of his own most used writing has come after some of his hardest lessons. He quotes Psalm 32:8, 9 (New Living Translation): "The Lord says, "I will guide you along the best

> Sometimes the Lord has to do quite a work in us before He can do the work He wants to do through us.

pathway for your life. Do not be like a senseless horse or mule that needs a bit and bridle to keep it under control." Bob Fitts has said that he hopes that writing good songs doesn't mean that you have to go through hard times, "but... I kind of think it does."

The Lord is the Master Potter.
He keeps working me over,
shaping and reshaping me.
Sometimes He has to break me first.
I must admit I dread those remodeling jobs.
But the truth is I'm lopsided and I leak.
I want to be a strong, beautiful vessel,
full of the praise and music and
glory of God. So I say,
go ahead, Lord;
fix me.

ƧƧƧƧƧ

Open the eyes of my heart Lord

Open the eyes of my heart

I want to see You

I want to see You

To see You high and lifted up

Shining in the light of Your glory

Pour out Your power and love

As we sing holy holy holy

Holy holy holy

I want to see You

(Paul Baloche)

―――

HOW THE SONG WAS BORN
Paul: Open the Eyes of My Heart

Of all my songs, it's amazed me how many people have responded to this one. I've received more emails and calls and letters and responses from churches saying, "This is the theme of our church this year. This is the theme of our conference. This is the cry of our hearts." Hearing people resonate with that same desire to say, "I've been in religion a long time and that's not enough. I want to know Him. I want to see God." "Lord, I want to wake up each day and be more aware of Your presence in my life. I want to see Your kingdom in the midst of this world, so I can be a part of it and do my part."

This song was inspired in part by Ephesians 1:18. The Apostle Paul was writing a letter to the Ephesians and he said, "I pray that the eyes of your heart would be enlightened."

That scripture stirred in my heart for a while. So, one morning while playing during a ministry time at my church, I began to sing that phrase over and over again: "Open the eyes of my heart Lord, open the eyes of my heart..." The whole song pretty much rolled off my tongue while I was prayerfully playing my guitar and singing out to Him.

Publishing and Promoting Your Songs

Craig Dunnagan, VP, Music Publishing and Church Resources, Integrity Music

Are you so foolish? After beginning in the Spirit, are you trying to attain your goal by human effort?

Galatians 3:3 (NIV)

We start pursuing God with no thought of gain or increased influence; we simply want to give our lives for Him and make our love for Him known in our songs. It's amazing how things get complicated as we get "older." God is the One who imparts gifts into our lives, but when we attain some level of accomplishment with those gifts, we often start trying to "figure out" the next steps of ministry and impact.

These tendencies are almost unavoidable in our culture, but God calls us to a higher place. The key is not to elevate the gifts by spending our energies hoping our efforts get noticed, but to spend them making sure God gets noticed through the gifts. We say worship is "all about Jesus," but our lives don't always reflect that. We're all (music publishers and record companies included) sometimes guilty of this loss of correct focus.

With that spiritual focus in mind, let's talk about getting your songs "published." First: "published" is often equated with signing your song to a music publisher. However, technically, a song is "published" when it has been duplicated beyond personal copies (copies for worship team or bulletin), performed in a public setting (worship service), displayed publicly (overhead projector), etc. Therefore, many writers have been published and don't realize it.

The role of publishers and record companies is to expand the access of songs. There's a common misconception that publishers and record companies create popular songs and worship leaders/artists. The truth is, we don't create momentum for ministry, but build a platform under already vibrant and active ministries. We don't create moves of God, we document them. A greater truth is that God doesn't need music publishers to spread His songs across the earth; He chooses them, like any other human vessel. If your music is impacting your city, region, denomination, etc. then it's likely we'll hear about it. That sounds like a simplistic answer to an evasive quest: publishing and recording. However, I can't tell you how often I hear about a person or a song from different places at the same time. It's like God is saying, 'Paul is ready for his songs to be heard by more people.' If God isn't your promoter, you're fighting a major uphill battle. He promotes the humble, sold-out servants who, like the psalmist David, would be just as satisfied singing their songs to Him on a hillside as they would in front of thousands of people.

1. Share your songs within your current sphere of influence. Opportunities start with relationships. If you're part of a denomination, share the songs that are really "working" in your congregation with your state music committee. If they love them, they'll likely share them with others and the song will take on a life outside your home

church. Create a fellowship of local worship leaders where you can share ideas and songs. Come with simple demos and chord charts or sheet music. If fellow worship leaders like your song, they'll try it in their churches. If it works there, where there's no personal incentive for the congregation to like it, then that song can work well in other churches.

2. Record and distribute a recording of your original songs. I tend to pay more attention to a well packaged recording from a local church than from an individual's demo. If the pastors and congregation believe in your ministry and songs enough to fund a recording, that speaks of endorsement from them and faithfulness from you. We've even asked for a letter of recommendation from the pastor or a staff minister. Once you have a respectable recording, send it to outlets such as Grassroots Music Distribution, WorshipMusic.com or Song Discovery. All of these gladly receive and review independent recordings and, in some cases, make the songs or products available to their constituents.

3. Attend Worship Conferences and Music Conferences. These are the best places to meet and develop relationships with nationally known worship leaders and songwriters. There may be song-sharing opportunities or contests where songs are submitted, judged and awarded. Examples: International Worship Institute, Purpose Driven Worship Conference, Seminars 4 Worship (Integrity Music) and others.

4. Engage in limited itinerant ministry. If God has given you excellent songs for the church, then share them in other congregations. This is assuming you have "presentational" skills that do the songs justice. When you're ready to do this, don't leave your home church. Stay anchored where your gifts were nurtured and encouraged in the first place. Stay near the well where your source of life and inspiration comes from. However, with the blessing of your leadership, pursue and accept invitations from other churches. This increases the opportunity for someone influential to hear about your songs and share your name or music with those who can give you a broader platform.

There are multitudes of ways your songs can be heard and sung. However, the above four are by far the best first steps that, from my experience, lead to songs gaining a wider platform.

Attitude Check

Some sincere Christians worry about their motivation in writing songs for the Lord. Yet we can't discuss songwriting without recognizing the potential *commerciality* of what we do. The writing and merchandising of Christian materials is unlike others, in that we're handling the word of God. But printing, recording and distribution cost money. If the publishers or record companies don't make a profit, they can't stay in business, in which case Bibles, books, song books and recordings will be hard to come by. Publishers and songwriters shouldn't have to apologize for making a living from what they do, any more than Christian pastors or carpenters. Paying our pastors and teachers is a scriptural premise, and it applies to other forms of ministry as well. But covetousness and greed are not acceptable in any Christian.

It comes down to heart attitude, doesn't it? If God has given us the ability to make a living from our gifts, let's be thankful and responsible, never letting money be the deciding factor over ministry. Let's pray over our calling, deal with our own hearts, and be sure that our motivation is as clean as we can make it. We're not writing, performing or leading worship in order to become rich and famous, but to be used by God. If success comes, we thank God for it, but we hold it lightly and try to be generous and humble about what we do with it. So don't be afraid to exercise your gift for fear you're doing it for the wrong reason, or you may become like the man Jesus told about who buried his talent and was punished for it. Our motives may vary from day to day— 80/20, 90/10, 50/50. That's not all bad. **Pray for purity and servanthood, and go ahead and write.**

Don't Quit Your Day Job

We saw someone wearing a tee shirt that said, "Quit Work. Make Music." Sounds like fun, but until you've reached the place where your songs are regularly

> If we had to wait until we were perfect in order to serve the Lord, nobody would ever do anything.

being published and recorded, *don't* give up your job to work full time on songwriting. We've seen people do this and bring financial disaster on themselves and their families. Remember, even King David, who was arguably the greatest songwriter in the Bible, didn't quit his day job. Even when publishers start using your material, it takes a while to build a solid catalogue that will bring in enough money to live on. In fact, very few ever make a full-time living from songwriting. So don't do anything rash. Work as steadily at your music as you can, and things will unfold for you gradually in God's timing, if He has called you to it in the first place. In the meantime, prepare yourself to be the very best you can be. Offer your talent to the Lord and let Him place you where He wants you.

Be the Best You Can Be

You may be content to keep your music as a hobby, but if you find you have a serious gift that is beginning to be recognized by others, our advice to you is to learn all you can as fast as you can. It will make the rest of your life easier and more fulfilling. Being really fluent in modern harmony can mean the difference between many years of soaring with your gift—or many years of slogging with it, always trying to figure it out instead of *knowing* what you're doing. It can be very frustrating to hear great music in your head but not know how to communicate it. What you don't know can hurt you. Whatever your musical ambitions may be, learn all you can. **The more you know, the better off you are.**

What's Your Calling?

Do you feel a specific sense of direction yet in your writing? This book focuses on worship songs, but we realize that many of our readers will also write other kinds of songs, from CCM to wholesome entertainment.

Paul has a very specific calling to write worship songs. That's what he is, a lead worshiper/songwriter, and his songs reflect his calling.

Jimmy and Carol felt early on that their calling was not so much to write for artists, although they have done some of that, but to write for churches to perform, and especially to write dramatic musicals (involving characters, dialog, etc.) and interactive musical events (involving minister/narrators and audience response.)

Their advice: If you decide to write musicals for the church, recognize that there are two drawbacks to this:

1. Although you record your musical with professionals, you're really writing for amateurs to perform, so you have to be careful about the level of difficulty. Doesn't sound very satisfying to the writer's ego, does it? But when we use the term *amateur*, we don't use it in a demeaning way. Although it does mean "someone who doesn't make a living from his work," it also has another meaning. The *ama* comes indirectly from the Latin *amare*, meaning "to love," and *amateur* means someone who does something for the love of it. That's not bad. There are lots of "amateurs" out there who are better than some professionals.

2. In writing musicals, realize that most of the songs you write will never be heard apart from the musical. There are, of course, certain songs within musicals, which we refer to as *takeaway songs* or *lifters*, that can stand alone. But most songs in musicals are *book songs*. They

carry detail about the plots and characters, further the action, and replace dialogue. For example, a song called "Nothin' Ever Happens Here in Galilee," from Jimmy and Carol's *The Witness*, sets the stage for the appearance of Jesus on the scene, but is unlikely to be sung apart from the musical. Or the emotional "Where Have the Children Gone?" will probably never be heard outside its setting in *Heal Our Land*.

But these songs served their purpose well.

So although the Owenses have some 250 published and recorded songs, about 70 percent of them are parts of their 12 musicals. But they're content with this. That has been their calling, and it's more satisfactory to see their musicals used than their individual songs. A musical is synergistic. That is, its effect is greater than the sum of its parts. The 15 or so songs of a musical, along with its story or narration, concentrate their power in a way that, as individual songs going their separate ways, they couldn't do.

Maybe you haven't felt a specific sense of direction yet, but be open for anything.

ჳჳჳჳ

•
My
soul,
God has
plans for you.
Never forget it.
They are personal
and specific plans.
Listen for the whisper.
Look for the signs. Follow
the arrows. Then once you
know the direction—and it may
not always be the one you would
choose—don't be obstinate. Having to
be disciplined is so time-wasting. And
so hard on the spiritual backsides.
Much better to let His
will be done.

ჳჳჳჳ

Making Demos

- Some publishers say you don't need to go to great expense to make a demo; a cassette will do, so long as it's *clear*.

Tom Kraeuter adds to this:

"True. But as one who has sat and listened to hundreds of songs that people submitted for possible publication in *Psalmist* magazine, I would say emphatically that the better the quality of the recording, the more favorably the song will be considered. No matter how unbiased people endeavor to be, the quality of the recording will influence their final judgment on the song."

- **Try for the best quality possible in your recording**. At the very least, use two inputs if you can, one for the voice and one for the instrument, or it may sound like one or the other is phoned in.

- **If you aren't a good singer, get someone to sing your demo for you,** preferably someone with a contemporary sound. Ask yourself: Is this a guitar-driven song or a piano-driven song? Find someone who can play it confidently and a singer who can communicate it well.

- **Avoid excessive stylizing** in the vocal performance. **State the melody clearly** at least the first time through.

- **Get the best feeling you can in the vocal.** Emotion is more important than technical perfection.

Placing Your Songs

Is it better to try and go through an established publisher or to self-publish? There are pros and cons. More people are using Christian music than ever before, but more people are *writing*, so the standard has been raised very high. Publishers are likely to invest only in writers with outstanding potential, both in talent and visibility. Major publishers may be hard to get to, but there are lots of small independent Christian labels springing up everywhere, who need good songs to get started. You might submit your material to them. It could be a win/win for both of you. But be sure they have the ability to record, publish, market and distribute your songs.

If you're an entrepreneur and have great faith in your talent, *a platform for visibility* and the wherewithal to do all that's needed, you might pray about self-publishing. The main thing is to get your songs heard at whatever level you can, large or small. The cream will rise to the top. And by that we're not implying that a major publisher/label is necessarily the top, at least from

God's viewpoint. If you make yourself the best songwriter/communicator you can be, the Lord will place you where you fit.

If you decide to submit your songs to publishers, do your homework first:

- Find a publisher or artist who does your kind of music.

- Put one or two songs on your demo, with your strongest song first.

- Enclose lead sheets (lyrics, melody and chords.) If you can't, send just lyrics.

- Enclose a self-addressed stamped envelope if you want your demo back.

- Put your name and info *on* the demo. Boxes and envelopes get lost.

- Never send anyone your only copy.

- Send a *brief* cover letter that tells the publisher who you are and what you want to do with your music. If he likes your work it can give him a feel for you as a person and establish a rapport between you.

Pay attention to the songs you've written that raise their heads above the others. Do people seem affected by this song? Do they rise to their feet when that one is sung? Are some moved to tears at one of your songs? If you have a song that your congregation *really, really* loves, it might help if your pastor gives you a letter saying so. If you have a *good* recording of your congregation singing your song, it might be better than a solo demo.

Here is a major key: Publishers are looking for songs that are congregationally tested.

- **Don't expect a critique** or even a reply unless your songs are accepted.

These songs will tell the publisher whether you have possibilities as a long-term songwriter. Publishers are looking not only for songs but for songwriters—people who can consistently write quality songs, people they can invest in. Make every song on a demo as strong as possible.

Some major Christian publishers no longer accept unsolicited material. That can be discouraging, but there are ways around that. Here are a few steps to take to increase your chances of getting your song heard by some major publishers:

If possible, attend worship conferences and concerts sponsored by well-known publishers. Come prepared with a few copies of your one- or two-song demo, with a cover letter, lead sheets, etc., as we mentioned above.

Politely pass on a copy to any representative or recording artist you can. Briefly tell them of your package which contains *two songs maximum.* Publishers and artists are much more willing to pop a CD in and listen to one or two songs than ten songs.

Tell them you don't expect a critique or a response, but ask if they would be willing to listen to the song and, if they feel it has merit, pass it on to the appropriate person at the record company. In nine out of ten cases, when a song gets accepted, there has been some kind of relational thing that gets the attention of the publisher.

Even though some major publishers no longer accept unsolicited submissions, you can still try. Write on the outside, "Attention: Song reviewer. Package contains a one- (or two-) song submission."

- When you find a publisher who is interested in your songs, **don't play hard-to-get;** he may not be all *that* interested. Until you have a good track record, you're really not in a position to make demands. Be satisfied with a standard contract, and glad to get it, at that. If you're an

Cast your bread upon the water. Sow your seed. Nothing ventured, nothing gained.

artist/songwriter with a strong track record or good potential visibility, a publisher/record label may be willing to negotiate something better for you.

- **Never sell your songs outright**. Normally you assign ownership of the song to the publisher. Their job is to see that your song is published and distributed, whether by print or recording or both. The publisher obtains international copyrights on the song and administrates it—that is, they issue licenses and collect the money from people who record or publish your material. After keeping their percentage, they see to it that you receive your share of these monies.

- Ask for a **reversion clause** in case the publisher fails to fulfill his obligation to get your song published (by either print or recording) within a reasonable length of time. Ownership of the copyright would then revert back to you.

- Your publishing company will belong to one or more of the **performing rights societies,** ASCAP, BMI or SESAC, and will help you decide which to join.

Briefly, this is the way the performing rights societies work: Music users, such as television and radio stations, obtain the right to play all the songs of the society's members by buying a license from the society. The societies then sample the logs of these stations and other users and allocate to the writers and publishers their shares of these monies.

CCLI

Before we move on, let's discuss an aspect of the music business unique to the Christian field. Christian Copyright Licensing, International (CCLI) has been a great blessing to many writers and owners of songs used in ministry. Under copyright law, permission is required from a copyright holder for the reproduction of a song. Think of the trouble this used to be for churches wanting to print worship choruses in their bulletins or project them on their screens. To remain legal and honest, someone was supposed to write each publisher for permission every time a copy of a song was made—an impossible task that rarely got done. This problem was solved by the formation of CCLI, an organization that represents hundreds of publishers and tens of thousands of their songs. For a modest annual fee, any church may make legal copies of song lyrics for congregational use. Churches report their use on a specified schedule, sampling is done, and royalties are paid to the participating publishers to share with the writers. It's a win-win situation; it saves the churches a lot of trouble and expense, and it keeps publishers in business and blesses songwriters with fair remuneration for their labors.

What I look for in a new congregational Worship Song

Craig Dunnagan, VP, Music Publishing and Church Resources, Integrity Music

When I'm listening to new songs from writers there's always a sense of anticipation. Could this be the next "Open the Eyes of My Heart" or "Here I Am To Worship"? It's a privilege to help writers take their Holy Spirit inspired ideas, craft them and then offer them like new born babies as gifts to worshippers wanting to express their hearts to the Lord in a fresh, exciting and accessible way. There are many paths to powerful worship songs but there are some key issues for me as a publisher that I consider.

203

When listening to songs for the first time I try to turn off my brain and turn on my heart. A song can break all the normal rules of songwriting but bear such a touch of God that you can't ignore it. There are many songs being used by God in the Church that are not perfect but are powerful. With all that said, let me share some key practical and spiritual considerations for new congregational worship songs:

Singable Melody —Is the melody in a *range* that the typical church member in the pew can sing? This range varies based on the key the song is written in. Also, are the *intervals and melodic flow* such that the person in the pew can feel comfortable with the song? A song too challenging melodically is sure to become a "solo perfor- mance" by the worship leader and team.

Accessible Lyrics—Does the lyric present a *clear and understand- able concept?* Is it *well written and crafted?* Does the lyric repre- sent a *unique expression of a universally beneficial and useful idea* such as scripture, expressions of praise, worship or prophetic statements that move people closer to aligning with the Word and will of God. Obscure ideas or complicated poetry that require expla- nations before the songs can even be presented, indicates that the writer was more interested in the "art" of the song than the "heart" of the song.

Memorable – A song can be easy to sing and accessible lyrically but be very ordinary. The incredible challenge in writing worship songs is to take singable melodies and accessible lyrics and craft them into an extraordinary and unique musical and spiritual event. Fresh expressions of worship, testimony or praise in a unique melodic or musical setting are what sink into my heart.

I'm not looking for good songs or even "great" songs; I'm looking for *transforming* songs. The songs our congregations embrace are adding to the liturgy of the Church. Let's give them songs that con- vey the Truth and bring us into life-changing encounters with God's Word and God's presence.

I see the Lord
And He is seated on the throne
The train of His robe
Is filling the heavens
I see the Lord
And He is shining like the sun
His eyes full of fire
His voice like the waters
Surrounding His throne
Are thousands singing
(Chorus)
Holy holy holy
Is the Lord God Almighty
Holy holy holy
Is the Lord
Holy holy holy
Is the Lord God Almighty
Holy holy holy
Is the Lord

(I See the Lord, by Paul Baloche)

CHAPTER 10
MUSIC THAT MINISTERS

Three Ministries

All of us Christians, whether we are songwriters, singers, preachers, teachers, or just disciples, are, in the truest sense, supposed to be ministers.

Maybe you haven't thought of yourself as a minister, but if you're a Christian, that's what the scripture says you are. Ephesians 4:11-12 (New King James Version) says, "And He Himself gave some to be apostles, some prophets, some evangelists, and some pastors and teachers, *for the equipping of the saints* (that's us—all of us Christians) *for the work of the ministry,* for the edifying of the body of Christ." As ministers we have three scriptural ministries to perform. And as songwriters, these are the things we write about:

- First, our ministry ***to the Lord,*** in our fellowship with Him, in praise, worship, prayer and obedience. We write songs for the church to use in this ministry.

- Second, our ministry *to one another,* as brothers and sisters in Christ. We're told to exhort, edify and encourage one another: "teaching and admonishing one another in psalms and hymns and spiritual songs"(Colossians 3:16). Remember the time A.A. Milne's Pooh Bear ate too much and got stuck in a rabbit hole? He knew he would have to wait there, perhaps for a long time, until he grew thin enough to get out. So his friends all gathered around and sang him "sustaining songs." That's music ministry.

- Third, our ministry *to the world* —that's evangelism. We're entrusted with the greatest message in the world, the Good News that God sent His Son to die for our sins and now offers the free gift of eternal life to all who receive Him.

In these three ministries—each with a separate purpose—we find ample subject matter for all the songs we might ever want to write. But it's amazing to see how their purposes flow together. As the church again learns to worship the Lord and minister to one another in love, more and more people are coming to Christ in church services. We still need evangelistic songs to preach the gospel out in the world where most of the lost are, but it's interesting that the songs we write for God's people to use in their ministries to the Lord and to one another often turn out to be our most powerful instruments of evangelism.

Worship Evangelism

An unconverted person among worshiping Christians doesn't have to hear a sermon to convince him that he needs the Lord. The Holy Spirit, inhabiting the praises of His people, convinces him of that. We've often seen more people come to Christ in worship times than in evangelistic services.

Pastor Jack Hayford

Pastor Jack started The Church On The Way in Van Nuys, California with eighteen people. Early on he started the practice of leading the congregation in worship. He also taught the people to pray with each other in small groups. On Sunday morning he almost always gave the invitation to receive Christ *before* the sermon, so the sermon could be directed toward teaching, "equipping the saints for the work of the ministry." As he closed the worship time, he would give a two-minute explanation of how to receive Christ, inviting people to respond in their seats, then come into the prayer room after the sermon for counselling. After eighteen years they found that 25,000 people had come forward to receive Christ. By then the church had grown into thousands and had launched a number of daughter churches. All this with the invitation given at the close of the worship segment, *before* the sermon!

Anointing Oil

Most of us will agree that the single most important quality we could hope for in a Christian song is the power of the Holy Spirit on it. We don't want our songs just to make people feel good; we want to see people converted, comforted, helped, strengthened and led into the presence of God.

What is it that invokes this presence, this power, on a mere song? It's the anointing of the Holy Spirit. But how do we get this anointing on our music? Let's look at what the Scriptures say:

Jesus said, "Out of the abundance of the heart the mouth speaks. A good man out of the good treasure of the heart brings forth good things" (Matthew 12:34). We are what we have become; our treasure is what we have treasured. What we "bring forth" in our writing can only be what is inside us, what we've put there.

By "good things" we don't mean only "religious things." Few of us devote all our time to prayer, meditation and devotional reading. But the Apostle Paul tells us what things to think on—things that are true, honest, just, pure, lovely, of good report, virtuous, praiseworthy; think on these things, he says. Every good and perfect gift comes from God. He gives us "richly all things to enjoy." (1 Timothy 6:17). There are many good things for us to fill our treasuries with that aren't specifically religious things. However, most of us probably spend far too little time in the treasury of the Word of God itself. Paul wrote, "Let the word of Christ dwell in you richly in all wisdom" (Colossians 3:16).

Richness in our message and music comes from what we've put into the mixing bowl of our minds and characters. A mind of depth and breadth will produce a message of substance. A beautiful and serene spirit will convey beauty and serenity. A soul hotly in touch with God will serve as a conduit for the fire of the Holy Spirit.

So, does it matter what we listen to? Absolutely. And what we watch, and what we read. If our writing is a subconscious product of what we take into our minds and spirits, it matters *a lot* what we put in there. People who allow themselves to be entertained by crude ideas and lewd people gradually lose bits and pieces of their character. And our character determines our output. As people who try to help lead others to the Throne of God, we have an obligation. There are certain "artists," writers and entertainers that we must keep out of our "greenhouse" because their influence pollutes whatever it touches.

Jesus told His disciples that the Comforter, the Holy Spirit, would bring to their remembrance all the things He had said to them. **If snatches of scripture containing guidance and insight flash into our minds at** appropriate times, it's because we've planted them there for the Holy Spirit to bring to our remembrance when we need them.

He will also "bring forth" the things of God as inspiration for the songs we're to write. **We are not just to write nice Christian sentiments; we're to let Him speak through us in our songs.** Surely this is what the Apostle meant about yielding our bodies a living sacrifice to God (Romans 12:1); our minds, our talents, our hands are yielded to Him for His purposes. This is the way to the anointing.

Buddy Owens, author of "The Way of a Worshiper"

Buddy is Jimmy and Carol's son. Formerly a V. P. with Maranatha! Music, he was General Editor of the NIV Worship Bible. He is now a pastor at Saddleback Church in Lake Forest, California and Editorial Director for Purpose Driven Ministries, with Senior Pastor Rick Warren. In Buddy's teaching to worship leaders and pastors at more than 40 Promise Keepers conferences, he has often keyed in on Colossians 3:16: Let the word of Christ dwell in you richly in all wisdom, teaching and admonishing one another in psalms, hymns and spiritual songs. There's no way a verse could be more targeted for worship leaders and songwriters. He says:

"**First,** *Let* **the word dwell in you richly:** You have a role to play, making your time, mind and heart available.

"**Then, Let the word** *dwell* **in you richly:** Not a quick visit; let it take residence, give it time and space.

"**Last, Let the word dwell in you** *richly***:** Soak it up like a tea bag in hot water, until it colors and flavors your whole life.

"*Then* **write your songs for the church, 'teaching them with psalms, hymns and spiritual songs.'"**

𝔍𝔍𝔍𝔍

Father, I need a bigger
measure of the Family creativity.
When I imagine the paeans of
praise in Heaven, I feel
embarrassed by the
little songs I offer
to the Church as
vehicles for worship.
But You understand that
I do the very best I can with
the measure of talent I've
been given. So Lord, give my
songs Your anointing. With
that they will become far
more than they really are.

𝔍𝔍𝔍𝔍

Selecting Songs for a Specific Occasion

As we said at the beginning of the book, **the qualities you strive for in writing worship songs are the same ones you look for in *selecting* them**. You will look for songs that are easy to learn, hard to forget, emotionally touching and spiritually powerful.

There are hundreds, even thousands, of titles to consider. It can become a mind-boggling process. Let's say you find one with an interesting title—this sounds like the *message* you're looking for. But—the tune is dull and unmemorable, or the words are trite and unlyrical, and the hooks are non-existant. Pass this one up. Your congregation may try to sing it because you ask them to and they're good sports (after all, they're a captive audience.) Then again, they may not. At any rate, they won't remember it, nor, if given the opportunity to vote, will they ask for it again.

But there are some other factors to consider in planning a worship set:

> Watch your congregation. If half of them are dutifully clapping to the beat while gazing around the room with their mouths shut, that song isn't working.

1. **What is the Holy Spirit saying to this congregation now?**

2. **What is the pastor ministering on in this service?** (This may or not be important. Some pastors prefer the songs to relate thematically to the sermon, while others feel that a good worship experience is all that's necessary.)

3. **Where are the people in their corporate experience, and what are they ready for now? Spiritually? Culturally?**

4. **What songs, and in what sequence, will best lead the people into an awareness of the Presence of God?** Choose songs that move progressively through the gates, into the courts, then into the Throne Room. (Psalm 100:4) Avoid mere musical variety for its own sake.

5. **Consider using at least one great hymn** of high praise, then select worship songs that relate to its theme.

6. **Know where you're aiming, but be ready to change as the Spirit leads.** A sensitive leader will on occasion go into a song that hadn't been planned, because the Holy Spirit is doing something unanticipated among the people and the leader feels the need to linger on this theme and let God do his work. This can only happen in cases where the leader is mature and able to minister and has the trust and

permission of the pastor. But if God wants to do something that we hadn't planned for, it would be a shame to tell him, "Sorry, Lord, but You can't do that. It isn't printed in our bulletin."

7. **The handoff. What will the pastor do when you finish the worship time?** He may want to continue in an unbroken stream of ministry. The handoff song should be carefully chosen to achieve this.

8. In all your praise and worship writing and leading, **don't forget Jesus.** Not every song needs to be about Him, but with all the recent emphasis on Old Testament patterns of worship and setting psalms to music, He sometimes gets left out. But the preaching of the cross and the name of Jesus are where the life-changing power is. All the symbolism of the Old Testament altar consisted of types and shadows of which Jesus is the fulfillment. (But who wants to live in shadows?) When you're putting together a worship service, give some thought to this. And when you're praying about what to write—**The church needs songs that:**

   1. Invoke the presence of God, to minister to and to be ministered to by Him.

   2. Declare the glory, authority and power of God.

   3. Acknowledge the faithful provision of God in every need.

   4. Acknowledge the *work of the Cross* for reconciliation and access to God.

   5. Respond to the *claims of the Cross* to all we have and are.

   6. Ask for God's blessing and intervention in our nation.

7. Ask for God's blessing and intervention in the nations of the world.

8. Declare our position and authority in Christ and wage spiritual warfare.

APPLICATION:

Whether you're presently a worship leader or not, plan a worship set, considering each of the questions above.

Hymns or Choruses?

Worship songs and hymns generally serve two different purposes. A worship chorus, with its more frequent repetition and built-in cries, has little room for more than one or two thoughts, and serves as a prolonged emotional expression of a moment's devotion. The great hymns, with their four or more verses, each treating a different aspect of the theme, are full of richness, sublime thoughts and doctrine. A century or more ago it was common for a Christian to own a Bible and a hymnbook, which he used not only in church, but as private devotional reading. Many a Christian owed much of his knowledge of doctrine to the hymns, which hammered the great truths metrically into his memory. This practice is rare today, and congregations that are served only a steady diet of short choruses sung over and over are being malnourished and robbed of a rich part of their heritage.

Matt Redman: The Big Picture

In many of the hymn books there are songs on so many aspects of the nature and character of God. Songs which embrace every season of the soul. Hymns which give the people of God a voice to express worship in so many different circumstances of the Christian life. Collected together these hymns paint a big and colorful picture of God and His kingdom. Let us too take us this call—for one thing, let us begin to 'mind the gaps'—to attend to some of the areas of theology and life of which the church does not have many songs to sing. This is not a task we can take on alone. We need to seek help from theologians, preachers and pastors—people who can help us identify some of these gaps, and even suggest ways we might go about filling them. There is a heightened call on all of us to bring honour to God, edification to the church and truth to the world by painting as big and as full a picture of our God in worship as we possibly can.

Bob Kauflin, Sovereign Grace Ministries:

Sometimes songwriters start to write songs before they have very much to say. We assume that an outpouring of emotion is all that's needed to write a great song. The best congregational songs contain biblical truths and then give us words to properly respond to those truths. Truth without emotion is dead orthodoxy. Emotion without truth is fanaticism and potentially idolatrous.

• •

Jimmy

Sometimes, when I begin to get complacent and think my lyrics are pretty good, I need to be jarred back to reality by an encounter with true greatness. This old hymn does it for me every time. Its glorious, ever-changing imagery makes my hair stand up, and its sheer craftsmanship makes me hang my head:

1. O worship the King, all glorious above
And gratefully sing His wonderful love;
Our Shield and Defender, the Ancient of Days,
Pavilioned in splendor, and girded with praise.

2. O tell of His might, O sing of His grace,
Whose robe is the light, whose canopy space!
His chariots of wrath the deep thunderclouds form,
And dark is His path on the wings of the storm.

3. Thy bountiful care what tongue can recite?
It breathes in the air, it shines in the light,
It streams from the hills, It descends to the plain,
And sweetly distills in the dew and the rain.

4. Frail children of dust, and feeble as frail,
In Thee do we trust, nor find Thee to fail:
Thy mercies how tender, how firm to the end,
Our Maker, Defender, Redeemer and Friend.

O Worship the King, Lyrics by Robert Grant, Music:
William Gardiner's Sacred Melodies, 1815

(Note in the above song how the ever changing *feeling* of the message dictates how we arrange, interpret and perform a song. You wouldn't sing verse 2 and verse 3 in the same tone of voice, would you? And do any of the lyrics suggest some chord substitutions? Constantly consider these things when you're working out your team's arrangements.)

Since worship songs have replaced the hymns in many churches, **couldn't we write some more worship songs that are deeper and richer in spiritual content?** Consider some of the great old hymns, such as "Fairest Lord Jesus" or "When I Survey the Wondrous Cross." Each consists of three

217

to five verses full of rich, meditative imagery and doctrine. Three or four minutes of repetition of a simple thought in a worship chorus may make us *feel* reverent, or nostalgic, or worshipful, but may not feed our spirits on the truths of the faith as the hymns do. In our opinion both are needed, but in balance.

We're not suggesting necessarily that you write in the hymn format, but maybe there is an alternative. Today there seems to be a trend toward three-section worship songs, which may be AABBCC, or ABCABC, or some such combination. We particularly like ABABCC— Verse 1, Chorus, Verse 2, Chorus, followed by a different chorus, higher and repeated, that celebrates what the first sections have sung about. This still serves the purpose of a worship chorus but gives room for a lot more content.

Martin Smith's "Shout to the North" (ABABCB) has three thoughtful verses interspersed with its celebratory choruses, plus a bridge that adds more food for thought. Delirious?'s recording of it stretches the form to ABABBCBBABBBB and three *tags*. (A tag is a repeated final line.) As a refreshing surprise, the first of that last string of B's is sung by children. See also Martin Smith's "Did You Feel the Mountains Tremble?" Lots of great content here. The church could use more songs like these. Ask the Lord if He wants you to write some.

> Shortly before his death at age 28, Keith Green "discovered" and recorded "Holy, Holy, Holy." He lay on Jimmy and Carol's living room carpet with tears flowing into his ears as he listened to the rough mix of himself singing it.

New Life for Old Hymns

Here's another idea you might pray about. **There are literally hundreds of old hymns out there that have fallen out of use because their music and their language have become outdated.** We don't mean the famous hymns, the great old classic ones. We mean hymns you probably wouldn't know, because they haven't been sung for decades. But the thoughts, the doctrine, the sentiments they express are timeless. **There's a wealth of thematic ideas there, waiting for someone to express them in new music and new words.** Some of them are lost treasures. With a little research you might find them in musty old hymnals. Might they be waiting for you?

But what about the *great* old hymns? Hymns such as "A Mighty Fortress," "Christ the Lord is Risen Today," "Praise to the Lord, the Almighty," "Crown Him With Many Crowns," "When I Survey the Wondrous Cross," "For All the Saints" and "My Jesus I Love Thee" still speak to us today, even to the young who have never heard them before. Those are a part of the fabric of western civilization, and they live on from generation to generation. Greatness is greatness in any century.

Some might say, "But our church doesn't use hymns. We have a contemporary praise service, with choruses." You might be surprised to see how moving some of these hymns can be when set to *appropriate* new arrangements.

Before you retire an old song, see if there is a way to make it useful. Find a new groove? Try new chord changes? Revise archaic language? This doesn't mean, of course, that you should take an old hymn and make a doo-wop song out of it, but we've heard some great guitar-driven Praise Band arrangements of old hymns. **You may find a way to set an old song to a new arrangement and help it find new life in the church today.**

Timeliness or Timelessness

It's possible to write a song that's perfectly correct in every respect, except that it's written in a style that's several decades out of date. Some songs, however, are timeless. With an occasional change of arrangement or style, they can go on for many years. Melody Green's beautiful "There is a Redeemer," for example, sounds as if it could have been written today, or 30 years ago, or 300 years ago. Place it alongside the Wesleys' hymns of the early Eighteenth Century and it feels like it belongs there. With its classic, hymnlike quality, this song is destined for long life.

Well then, should we avoid writing in the popular styles of our own day because the songs won't last? Not at all. But let's do it in ways that will give our songs as much longevity as possible (such as using strong melodies) and with the understanding that we may not be writing for posterity but for our time only. Much contemporary Christian music will, in time, prove to have been temporary Christian music. **When times change and musical styles become obsolete, let's have the grace to let them go.**

Worship for Kids

In writing songs for kids to sing, the *basic* principles are the same, but there are certain other things to consider, depending on the age of the children we expect to sing our songs.

1. **Range.** Little kids, say three to five years old, have limited ranges. Keep the songs within a range of about middle C up to A or B. Even "Jesus Loves Me, This I Know" is a bit of a stretch for little kids. Some of them do "creative things" with the melody simply because they don't have that octave range the song requires.

    *   As they get older their range increases quickly. First-to-third graders can sing from C to C (with maybe a stretch on short notes up to D).

- By the time they are in grades 4 to 6, many kids may have a broader range than they will have as adults, say from low B♭ to high F, even G. But they need to be trained and vocalized to use the head tones on the high end.

- Junior high is the critical age, especially for boys. As they reach puberty they don't know what to expect their voices to do. They may crack and croak, embarrassing them to the point they don't want to sing. This is the hardest age to work with.

- High school kids, properly trained, can sing some fairly adult stuff.

2. **Melodies.** Try to keep little children's melodies especially simple and repetitive, hooky and easy to memorize.

3. **Lyrics.** Since little ones can't read, the lyrics shouldn't be too long for them to memorize. They might forget the words in performance.

4. **Vocabulary.** Lyrically, you want to write things a child would say, the way a child would say them. Check your lyrics for words too sophisticated for the age you're writing for.

5. **Concepts.** Don't get too abstract or symbolic with kids either. "Jesus loves me, this I know" is fine, but "His heart burns for me," or "I am swallowed up in His love," or some other such transcendent concept is beyond the ability of most kids to comprehend. Nor would it be believable coming from them.

Don't have little kids sing things like, "I was sinking deep in sin." (A three-year old?) Or, "Jesus set me free." Free from what? Most little kids have no concept of needing to be set free from anything yet.

6. **Theology.** Try not to get too theological with little kids. An elementary school child doesn't need to comprehend all the details of the atonement, for example. A four year old can understand that she has a naughty heart and Jesus will hear her prayers and come into her life and forgive her and help her to be good. But she doesn't need to be burdened with the traumatic concept that it was because she was naughty that Jesus had to suffer and die on the cross. When a little heart is open to the Lord, the Holy Spirit will reveal deeper aspects of truth as the child is able to grasp and to bear it.

7. **Difficulty level.** Kids are capable of a lot more than we sometimes expect of them. Rhythmically, they can do the most complex syncopation if they're properly directed. Maybe they can't read, but they can sing back to you almost anything they can hear.

   • A good way to teach them is to sing the phrase to them, then have them *say* the words over and over rhythmically until they can all say the line exactly together, with all the accents and inflections in place. Only then do you have them sing the line together a few times until it's clean.

   • When they get a little older you can add another step to the process. First have them *clap* the rhythm of the words together over and over until all the claps are together, then have them say the words, then sing them. This may take some experimentation, though, to see if your kids are ready for the clapping part; they may not be that coordinated yet. (This works for adult vocal groups too. It's fun, and it saves wear and tear on the voices.)

8. **Musical quality.** Kids deserve better music than a lot of the ditties that are written for them. Nowadays before they're out of the nursery they're already out of nursery rhymes and enjoying a higher

level of music than we did as kids, including the wonderful symphonic background music in TV reruns of *E.T.* and the like. So we don't need to write down to children too much.

9. **Remember your audience.** You're writing not only for kids to sing, but for adults to enjoy hearing them sing. The kids are being taught and stretched and blessed, but don't forget the doting parents who love hearing and seeing their adorable little ones perform.

> ### Cute
> If little kids are anything, they are cute. So write things that teach and nurture them, but also write cute things for them to sing and say. Writing for kids can be fun as well as rewarding, both for us and for them.

. . . .

Jimmy and Carol
Ants'hillvania

Occasionally the Lord lets writers hear some little vignette of how their music is used, and it's always great when that happens. A man recently told Jimmy and Carol: "I was leaving my wife and family, bags packed, on the way out the door. I peeked into my little boy's room and he motioned me in and patted his bed for me to sit down. He looked at me with his sad eyes and sang me two lines from Ants'hillvania: 'We'll miss ya, we really will miss ya. Come on home.' That did it. I'm still home, twenty years later." That man became a pastor and served until he went to be with the Lord this year.

Set to early cartoon-style music, *Ants'hillvania* is the story of a young ant named Antony, who wants to be an Independ-ant. He gets his inherit-ants and goes out into the big wide world to become rich and famous. He learns his lessons along the way and comes home as a Repent-ant, as his father shouts, "Kill the fatted aphid! My son has returned!" The musical, written with Cherry Boone O'Neill, got Dove and Grammy nominations as "Best Recording for Children" and, with its sequel, has recently been re-released by Sparrow Records.

Extra Techniques to Consider

Lining. Here's a technique you might want to try in your writing: it's called *lining.* It's very effective in situations where the congregation doesn't have access to the words and music. It has been used in many cultures, from ancient times to today, in Bible times, in the early American colonies where they had no hymn books, in tribal cultures with no written language. The leader sings a line at a time and the singers sing it after him or her. Sounds boring? Wait till you hear it done with a good solid groove. Think of that chant the Marines use in their marching drills, where the drill instructor shout-sings "I don't know but I've been told ..." and the troops sing each line after him. We can think of few worship songs done that way: "Victory Chant" (Hail, Jesus, you're my King!") and the verses of "You're Worthy of My Praise" and "Revival Fire Fall." There's room for more. Here is the form, used in Jimmy and Carol's "The Lord Rules!" from *Heal Our Land*:

The Lord rules (The Lord rules)
In power and might (In power and might)
The Lord rules (The Lord rules)
In glory and light (in glory and light)
In majesty (majesty) honor (honor)
Glory (glory) power (power)
The Lord rules (The Lord rules)
For ever! (for ever!) For ever! (For ever!)
And our God rules (And our God rules)
In the kingdom of men (In the kingdom of men)
And His is the power (And His is the power)
To raise up (To raise up)
To pull down (To pull down)
For He is the Lord (For He is the Lord)
Of all nations! (Of all nations!)
(Shout) God rules! (God rules!) God rules! (God rules!)

Call and Response. A similar device, called *Call and Response*, is found in Psalm 136, in which the leader sings different words to each line but is answered each time by the congregation with the same words, "His love endures forever." Chris Tomlin's "Forever" is based on this scripture. Jamie Owens Collins also used this device in "The Battle Belongs to the Lord."

(Verse 1)
In heavenly armor we'll enter the land
the battle belongs to the Lord
No weapon that's fashioned against us will stand
the battle belongs to the Lord

(Chorus)
We sing glory, honor,
Power and strength to the Lord
We sing glory, honor
Power and strength to the Lord!

(Verse 2)
When the power of darkness comes in like a flood
The battle belongs to the Lord
He's raised up a standard, the power of His blood
The battle belongs to the Lord.

(Verse 3)
When the enemy presses in hard do not fear
The battle belongs to the Lord
Take courage my friend, your redemption is near
The battle belongs to the Lord

II Corinthians 10:4:

The weapons of our warfare are not physical, but they are mighty before God for the overthrow of strongholds.

225

ᴣᴣᴣᴣ

God knows that, in this
chaotic world,
we need
every
means
of victory
we can find.
God has provided what we need:
The saving blood of the cross
The power of His name
The sword of His Spirit
And the shield of faith.
These assure us that
the battle is
not really
ours.
It is
His.
And He is right there,
armed and ready.

ᴣᴣᴣᴣ

CODA
GO FOR IT!

Scriptural Roots

So, you feel called to write songs for worship? It's a noble calling, and it has its roots deep in scripture. In Old Testament times being in a worship team was taken very seriously. Only the Levites were privileged to do it. They had to undergo special training and purification, and they were supported by the tithes of the people.

King David, "the Sweet Psalmist of Israel," was not only a great singer but a great songwriter as well. (He wrote over half of the Psalms.) David brought joy and exuberance to the worship—dancing, singing and playing the harp. Those harps were body instruments, more like guitars than what we call harps today.

While they had quiet worship music, 2 Samuel 6:5 tells us David and the whole house of Israel celebrated with all their might before the Lord, with lutes and pipes and trumpets and tambourines and cymbals and organs and lyres and harps. Nehemiah 12 describes a tremendous worship service, with choirs and worship bands, and says the sound of it could be heard far away.

The introduction to Psalm 7 in the Amplified Bible reads, "An Ode of David, (probably) in a wild, irregular, enthusiastic strain, which he sang to the Lord …" Habakkuk used the same form (called a *shiggaion)* in chapter 3: "a prayer of Habakkuk the prophet, set to wild, enthusiastic and triumphal music!" So if anyone gives you a bad time about your exuberant praise music, tell them to look it up in the Bible. Psalm 33:3 says "Play skillfully, with a loud noise." Of course, loud is relative. That was written before they had amplifiers capable of causing permanent ear damage.

When King Hezekiah restored the Temple worship, the scripture tells us in 2 Chronicles 29:

> Then he stationed the Levites in the house of the Lord with cymbals, with stringed instruments and with harps, according to the command of David... *for thus was the commandment of the Lord by His prophets.*

The idea of music in worship was God's in the first place.

All of that, of course, is from the Old Testament. You don't find much about music in the New Testament, partly because the new believers in Christ weren't trying to start a new religion. They worshiped in the temple, with all its music, and in the synagogues, and met together from house to house, until they were kicked out of synagogues, persecuted and scattered abroad (Acts 8:1). Being persecuted and in hiding is not exactly conducive to establishing a new music tradition, but it's interesting to speculate what the music of the early church might have sounded like when they were free to do it as they liked.

As the gospel spread throughout the world and Gentiles became Christians, they probably sang to the Lord and about the Lord in the music of their own cultures. By the end of the New Testament there wasn't as yet any new form of "Christian" music that we know of. So the tradition continues to evolve. In the two millennia since the New Testament era, Christian music has gone through as many variations as there have been cultures, from plainchant to anthems to rock, salsa and reggae. So what we have today comes from a long line of tradition, adapted to our own current culture.

Our ministry of worship today is still serious stuff. The call to excellence of what we offer to God hasn't changed. We don't have to be perfect, but we have to be as good as we can possibly be. No last minute rushing in to the service unrehearsed, trying to ad lib a few garage band arrangements.

Worship leaders still offer the incense of prayer and worship to the Lord and to the congregation. Songwriters provide the incense. Make it as pure and sweet and joyful as you can. This work is still holy.

The Origins of Contemporary Christian Music

If you're writing and ministering in contemporary Worship, it might be helpful to know some of the roots of the movement. The principle of using current popular music styles in Christian music is centuries old, but it had fallen into disuse in the first half of the Twentieth Century. Evangelical church music was frozen in a time warp. Churches usually had an organ, a piano, a choir and a few soloists, singing old hymns, anthems, religious art songs and gospel songs in the quaint archaic styles of the 19th Century. Bible teaching radio broadcasts presented male quartets that sang all four verses of these hymns and outdated gospel songs in incessant simplistic four-part harmony. Some Bible Belt churches used Southern Gospel music along with some simple congregational choruses, while black congregations enjoyed their own unique styles. There was a genre called "Singspiration," but it bore little resemblance to what the man on the street was listening to. Few understood the concept of "worship" as we now know it—leading the congregation together in singing songs *to* the Lord. Certain instruments were not welcome in church: saxophones were considered especially worldly, and drums were definitely of the devil. There was little there that people not raised in church tradition could relate to.

In the early 1950's a few Christian musicians began to experiment with a radical concept, that of trying again to communicate the gospel in musical styles the unchurched could identify with. A Salvation Army group called "Joy Strings" introduced Christian folk music, some brave Catholics created the "folk mass," John W. Peterson and Audrey Mieir wrote gospel songs with modern harmonies, and an innovative young student named Ralph Carmichael got himself into trouble with Bible college officials by setting hymns to big band jazz. He later became, for a time, the pace setter in Christian music.

The early efforts of many of these pioneers were met with opposition in parts of the church, but gradually there was some progress. The first significant Christian music recordings were made and the tamest of these began to get played on Christian radio stations. By the early 60's the atmosphere was changing, and some high quality music was being done. At first it was accompanied mostly by strings, then acoustic guitars sneaked in, still with no drums. A line was crossed in 1965 when Ralph Carmichael introduced some greatly toned-down"Surfer" type music in a Billy Graham movie about teens, called "The Restless Ones." It was acceptable in a film score, especially with the Billy Graham Evangelistic Association name attached to it, but it would be several years before this type of music would be welcome in many churches, even in the youth department. The breakthrough came in the late 60's with the Jesus Movement, when a new generation of young people were swept into the church in a great move of the Holy Spirit, bringing their music with them, drums, electric guitars and all. The term "Contemporary Christian Sound" was coined in 1967 to define what was being done. (It was the subtitle on the first Jimmy Owens Singers album, on Word Records.) Bill and Gloria Gaither linked together the Southern Gospel and Contemporary Christian Music fields and helped boost many artists into prominence.

Learning from the Past

We mentioned earlier the principle of writing Christian songs in the popular styles of the day. John and Charles Wesley did it in the 18th Century, and Martin Luther about two hundred years before them. George Frederick Handel did it, too, in the eighteenth century, though not in the style of the parlor but of the concert hall. He borrowed freely from himself in setting the scriptures to music for *Messiah,* using a number of tunes he had composed previously for other purposes. One of his great sacred choruses had originally been a tune about a silly goose. *Messiah* was at first banned and boycotted by many churches. Unlike Bach, who was primarily a church musician, Handel was best known as a composer of operas, a field many in the church considered worldly. So some people thought that *Messiah* was not worthy of association with the Holy Scriptures.

Pop Music in the Bible?

Speaking of pop music not being worthy of association with the scriptures: you may be surprised to know that some of the scriptures themselves were probably originally set to pop music. When you see the term, "To the Chief Musician," in the Psalms, it's often followed by an instruction from the lyricist, explaining how he wants the Psalm set to music.

The Amplified Bible tells us that the chief musician was instructed to set Psalms 45 and 69 "to the tune of 'Lilies' (probably a popular air)." The New Living Translation calls 'Lilies' "a love song." Asaph used the same tune for Psalm 80.

Apparently one of the top hits of the day was a song called "Do Not Destroy." David specified its tune for Psalms 57, 58 and 59, and Asaph used it for Psalm 75. David chose three other popular tunes, for Psalms 22, 56 and 60. (See the Amplified Bible.)

King David's Psalm 8, (O Lord our Lord, how majestic is your name in all the earth!) was, according to the Amplified Bible, to be "set to a Philistine lute, or (possibly) to a particular Hittite tune." The same instructions were given by Asaph for Psalm 81 and by the sons of Korah for Psalm 84. Whichever it may be, this was not a "religious" style. The Philistines were arch-enemies of the Israelites, and the Hittites were a heathen people only partially subjugated by Israel! God had warned Israel against worshipping their gods but apparently had no problem with co-opting their musical styles. So what's this about pop music not being worthy of association with the Holy Scriptures?

Different Strokes

Let's digress for a moment to consider a principle. In the vast diversity of religious expression, some people prefer to keep their religious lives separate from their everyday experience. Their lives are compartmentalized into religious and secular sections. The religious compartment contains a special "religioso" music, perhaps precious to them, that has little to do with the way they live and think in their everyday experience, and they feel uncomfortable in letting the compartments mix. They find a haven of rest and peace in this religious compartment, and it's very meaningful to them. Others, however, don't keep their spiritual expression in an isolated compartment; the music of their daily lives is the music of their spiritual lives. The Apostle Paul, in Romans 14:5, says that some think one day is more holy than another, while others think every day is alike. In the same manner, one person may maintain a compartmentalized existence while another lets all of life run together before the Lord—all of it is sacred. One way is not necessarily better than the other, and both believers may love God equally. For many in the latter category, happy blues-style music has become an integral part of their lives and so fits naturally into their religious expression.

Even so, be careful. Always use discretion in the way the message and the music work together. These are not songs about the Throne but about walking with the Lord or fighting His battles on earth. It's very easy to get so caught up in the fun of the music that the "praise service" becomes a fleshly emotional binge, but if the music team is under mature spiritual leadership, it can be a refreshing experience. (See 160, on Appropriateness.)

Watch for New Directions

As you write, stay alert to current trends. The cutting edge today seems to tend toward younger, more guitar-driven music—rawer, more garage-band-like in style and with a more overt cry of worship, adoration and commitment. Serious young Christians don't want to play at religion—they're interested in "extreme" Christianity and their music expresses it. Also, today's "melody vacuum" has created a hunger that is leading many to revisit the more musical styles of the 70's. How much of this will filter into mainstream adult Sunday worship remains to be seen.

Many churches today offer a choice of the Traditional Service or the Con-

Changing Times

As with most music, Praise and Worship music is in a constant state of change.

temporary Service (Some call it the Praise Band Service), and some have gone to what they call the Blended Service, a combination of both. (When the three of us were teaching in Singapore, our School of Music Ministries was hosted by Wesley Methodist, a large church that offered simultaneously both liturgical services and contemporary charismatic services. One Sunday morning a Chinese gentleman asked us, "Which way is the jolly service?" An apt description for a joy-filled, free-spirited time of worship.)

Another factor in the progression of worship music is the great success of the Promise Keepers movement. Several million men in arenas and stadiums have been led into a new experience in worship through contemporary music. Many of them, including many pastors, have gone back to their churches and become dissatisfied with the status quo. Many a church music department has been affected, if not outright overhauled as a result.

Be aware, though, of another trend, a disturbing trend. There are spiritually insensitive "praise bands" that get carried away with the fun of the music until it becomes rock for rock's sake. Some can conduct an entire "worship service" and never once approach a sense of *reverence*. To inflict this on a captive congregation is an act of aggression, like disturbing the peace. The church becomes an ideological battleground. Some people, not just the old, in their hunger for a true worship experience, leave and go to more formal churches where the sense of adoration of the majesty of God has not been lost.

The Way of the Visionary

There have always been true visionaries—those who catch sight of a new move of God before others see it. The visionary feels a great urge to *do* that thing the Lord has shown him—and do it *right now*. So he starts out boldly and soon finds himself the target of sticks and stones hurled by those who don't understand.

Stories abound about the church's resistance to new music forms:

- The first monk who experimented with part-singing was excommunicated.

- J. S. Bach almost lost his job as a church musician because some thought his music was unsuitable.

There have been some weird excesses that seem amusing to us today.

- In 1715 John Tufts tried to do something about the sad state of hymn singing in the Puritan church. Since musical instruments had been forbidden, everyone just sang the psalms (only the psalms were allowed) together without regard to the *time* or the *pitch* of anyone else. "Some sang too high," Tufts wrote, while others sang "too low, and most too long." When Tufts proposed that they all sing together, he stirred up a storm. The older Puritans said unison singing "robbed praise of its individuality and threatened them with the religious formalism they had rejected under the Church of England." It would be "a ceremony without unction or the inspiration of divine grace," "Papish," and "a worshiping of the devil." When one congregation persisted in the New Way, some parishioners put cotton in their ears.

- In 19th Century Scotland, Ira Sankey, Evangelist D.L. Moody's great song leader, was vilified by some for writing "human hymns" with newly composed lyrics instead of new tunes for the Psalms of the Bible, and for having the audacity to draw attention to himself by singing them as solos.

- Moody also caused a furor by having the singing accompanied by the hall's great pipe organ. One woman stormed out of the meeting shouting, "Och! It's the divil's instrument! There's a demon in ivery pipe!"

Want some more? Take a look at this: (Thanks to the Worship-and-Arts Network)

Top Ten reasons for Opposing the New Music Trend

Adapted from a statement directed against the use of *hymns*, in 1723

1. It is too new, like an unknown language.

2. It is not as melodious as the more established style.

3. There are so many songs that it is impossible to learn them all.

4. It creates disturbances and causes people to act in an indecent and disorderly manner.

5. It places too much emphasis on instrumental music rather than on godly lyrics.

6. The lyrics are often worldly, even blasphemous.

7. It is not needed, since preceding generations have gone to heaven without it.

9. It monopolizes the Christian's time and encourages them to stay out late.

10. These new musicians are young upstarts, and some of them are lewd and loose persons.

Even in our own time, those of us who have tried to change church music have often been misunderstood. The way of the innovator has not always been easy. Of course, willingness to persevere in the face of criticism sometimes is laudable. Criticism does have some value as a gauge: if we're getting no criticism at all, even from the "staid guardians of sterile orthodoxy," as A.W. Tozer called them, we probably aren't accomplishing much that's fresh and new and powerful. On the other hand, if we're getting a lot—especially from those who have walked with the Lord much longer than we have—maybe we need to back up a bit and listen. There's always the possibility we've gone too far too fast and we're over the line. Jimmy says, "Been there. Done that." He has memories from his younger, experimental days, of elders complaining to the pastor, "It sounds like a nightclub in here!"

The Lone Ranger Bites the Dust

The secret to being a successful innovator in Christian music lies largely in attitude. (We're talking now about true Spirit-led *innovation*, which means doing something new, not just blindly copying the latest rebellious fad and putting a Christian label on it, as some have done. The scripture tells us to "reprove the unfruitful works of darkness," not imitate them.) If the visionary says to himself, "I'm gonna do *my* kind of music *my* way (for the Lord, of course) and if the church doesn't 'understand' my music, I'll do it without them; I don't need anyone but Jesus, anyway"—he will fail. He will be perceived as a maverick and his attempts won't be supported. The Lone Ranger will bite the dust. (Eph. 5:11).

As Christians, we are all parts of the Body of Christ, and what we do in his name affects the world's perception of Christianity, reflects on the church and has implications wider than our own careers. A detached body part moving around by itself is the stuff of horror movies.

The truth is, he does need the church. Whatever we do in ministry must not be on our own. This doesn't mean we have to ask permission from some church authority every time we write a song, but it does imply an accountability and a willingness to accept correction on matters of doctrine and practice.

On the other hand, if he goes about it in the right spirit, the visionary has the opportunity to bring the church along with him into an understanding of what God has shown him. Of course, this takes patience. He'll need to slow down at times and wait for the church to catch up. Occasionally he'll take a leap that's just too broad for those without his vision to follow. When this happens, he will have to retrace his steps, rejoin his followers, maybe even apologize, do some explaining and teaching and then coax them along step by step until they, too, see his vision.

Besides patience he'll need love—a genuine love and respect for the church. He'll need to listen to wise counsel. He'll need forbearance—the Bible tells us to forbear one another (this could be translated "put up with one another"). And he will need faith—faith that if God has shown him something, God can also show it to others; and faith in the others, that they'll be able to see it when it's shown to them.

The innovator must forget the notion that he is personally responsible for making something happen. If God has set something in motion, God is responsible to make it happen. The visionary is responsible only to do what God directs him to do.

Thank God for the visionaries—the people who strive to see and hear and do the will of God even at the cost of being misunderstood, who put ministry first and are not corrupted by commercialism. They are on the cutting edge, and without them no real progress is ever made.

Be a Voice for God

Any of our voices is important only as it says what God is saying. "If any one speaks, he should do it as one speaking the very words of God." (1 Peter 4:11 NIV). Jesus said that He spoke to the world those things that He heard from the Father, and He did only those things that He saw the

Father doing. Not seeing and hearing as well as Jesus did, we still, no doubt, say a lot of things on our own. But when we're listening and watching very attentively, when we really do sense, see and hear something the Spirit is saying and then repeat it by means of our craft, we may find an astonishing difference in the way our work is received and used.

God didn't stop speaking to men after the canon of Scripture was complete. While we certainly don't equate the continuing "word of the Spirit" with the inspiration of the Scriptures, we do believe He speaks today by His Spirit *through* the Scriptures. None of these things we hear the Spirit saying to the church are new truths; they've been there in His Word all the time. It's just that He's currently drawing the church's attention to them. He lays fresh emphasis on certain portions of His Word in different stages of the lives of individuals, congregations and the church at large. He tells His listening intercessors what to pray for. He gives visionaries new paradigms of ministry. He shows His pastors which pastures to lead His people into next.

Most of what we hear God saying comes through other voices: a concensus of what responsible Christian leaders at large are saying they are hearing from Him. Then, as we pray, we may hear God saying in our own spirits, maybe not in words but in certainties, "This is what I want you to say; study it and write it for the church to share through your music." That's when songwriting becomes prophetic.

You don't have to have a special word from the Lord to write evangelistic or worship songs. But we do advise you to be alert for those *special* times when God lets you know He has something specific for you to say—now . . . on *this* subject . . . in *this* song or musical. It may come as you read His word or pray or meditate, or as you take your part in the life of the congregation. He isn't speaking to you alone about things no one else is hearing. It's precisely because others are listening too that they can say, "Why, that's exactly what the Spirit of God has been saying to me. I've been looking for songs that express that message. Thank God you wrote that!"

On the other hand, it's possible that God may sometimes lead you to write something few want to hear. A song calling for personal sacrifice may not be a runaway success in the marketplace. It's been said that the great majority of Christian books sold have to do with personal happiness: how *I* can be successful and blessed—spiritually, financially and emotionally. (We're not suggesting this is wrong—the great hero of faith George Mueller once said his first task each day was to get his soul happy, implying that only then could he be up to the tasks the Lord had for him.) And how many "hit" Christian songs do you know that call people to give, or to leave it all behind and go where God calls? Not all biblical prophets were received gladly by everyone either. Some were persecuted, but they delivered the word God gave them. If you're sure the Lord is leading you to write such a message, be obedient. God doesn't hold us responsible for success, but for faithfulness.

This, then is the greatest secret we have to leave with you, whether you're a preacher, a teacher, a songwriter or whatever God has called you to do:

Hear what the Holy Spirit is saying and let Him say it through you.

May God help us to
recognize His presence
when He comes to
move in our
service.
Sometimes
we are so busy
with our predesigned
program, we forget to
watch and listen for
the Holy Spirit.
How poor we
are if we
miss His
move.
Invoking His
wonder-working
Presence is what we're
really here for, isn't it?

> When people express themselves directly to the Lord in worship, God answers Spirit to spirit.

He is here, He is here
He is moving among us
He is here, He is here
As we gather in His name
He is here, He is here
And He wants to work a wonder
He is here as we gather in His name

He is Lord, He is Lord
Let us worship before Him
He is Lord, He is Lord
As we gather in His name
He is Lord, He is Lord
Let us praise and adore Him
Yesterday and today and for evermore the same

(Here is Here, by Jimmy Owens)

A New Day

In many churches music is finally being recognized and given its proper place in ministry. No longer is it just "the preliminaries," but an integral part of the worship. Many churches now have Ministers of Worship, not only to oversee the music department but to lead the congregation in expressing themselves to the Lord. The typical worship time in many such churches is an unbroken twenty to forty minutes, after which a smooth transition is made right into the sermon. The whole service is a seamless act of worship, including the offering. Most of the music is less performance oriented, and more congregational.

In churches that have learned to lead the congregation into personal, biblical worship, it's amazing to see how many people are receiving Christ in worship services. Many unconverted people are so drawn by the sense of the presence of the Holy Spirit inhabiting the praises of his people, that they begin to express their own hearts to the Lord. God gives them peace, and they begin a new life in Christ. **That simple worship song has become a powerful tool of evangelism.**

ༀༀༀༀ

God never intended
praise to be
simply a
minor part
of a service,
written down and
mumbled in unison,
without understanding,
or phrases repetitiously
and mindlessly sung. Whe-
ther it is the liturgy or the
spontaneous worship ser-
vice, we are meant to
enter into it with
the whole heart,
as if that is
what we
were
created
to do.
Because it is.
Lord, let my worship
rise like incense, touching Your
heart, bringing You joy, perfuming Your throne.

ༀༀༀༀ

A Worldwide Phenomenon

Because of our modern means of travel and communication the world has grown smaller. **The musical worship tradition with praise bands and worship "choruses" is now perhaps one of the most widespread forms in church history.**

Get into a Christian's car in almost any international city, and he's likely to pop in a recording by your favorite worship leader. Visit a few churches there and you're likely to find synthesizers, electric guitars, bass guitars, drums and vocal groups, singing the same worship songs we sing in our churches, along with new ones of their own.

Frank Fortunato reported recently from Mongolia, "The Western pop sounds dominate the youth culture as well as the worship services in the young Mongolian church." Mongolia?! That's the uttermost part of the earth!

Of course there are isolated pockets in the world that Western Civilization has not touched, or nations where despotic religions or tyrannical governments isolate their people. But in the former Soviet Union, the United Kingdom, Western Europe, Australasia, Africa, the Americas, on islands in the Caribbean and the Pacific and in much of Asia, praise and worship music as we know it is nearly universal. You'll hear different languages and refreshing local ethnic flavors, but the spirit is the same.

The Awesome Power of Music

Many of us are aware of the mood-influencing power of music. Grocery stores play background music that stimulates buying—doctors' offices play calming music—youth fashion shops play loud rock that attracts the young and the cool—Mozart supposedly stimulates learning abilities. Music was known to be therapeutic even in Old Testament times. When King Saul was visited by "an evil spirit from the Lord" he would call for David, whose harp playing would drive the spirit out (1Samuel 16:23). Elisha summoned a minstrel to aid in his prophesying (2 Kings 3:15).

But few have really understood the incredible power of music to change the world.

- Plato understood the power of music when he wrote, "Give me the making of the songs of a nation, and I care not who makes its laws; I will control its people."

- Martin Luther understood it when he wrote, "Music is a fair and glorious gift of God. I am strongly persuaded that after theology, there is no art which can be placed on the level with music. The devil flees before the sound of music almost as much as before the word of God."

Bear with us if we seem to digress, your Honor. We want to change direction for a few moments, but you'll soon see where we're heading, and we'll make our case. We want to talk about…The Beatles.

In a book on worship songs?

Yes, because they prove our point about changing the world. They were together for only seven years, yet their music filled the last third of the 20th Century and their influence continues strong into the next. Their melodies have been recorded by symphony orchestras, baroque chamber groups, easy listening strings, and even on music boxes as lullabies for babies. Harmonically, they liberated many rockers from the tyranny of three-triad monotony. In the end, sad to say, the Beatles, having captivated the hearts of a generation with their delightful, relatively innocent mischief, embraced hallucinogens and gurus, leading many with them down a dark path. But along the way they changed the world. Literally.

- Early in the new millennium *USA Today* and *CNN News* headlined: *"The 100 Events that Shifted History,* a list of the top news stories of the 20th Century, as determined by a survey of 67 journalists and historians."* Standing at number 58, lower in rank than the bombing of Hiroshima and the first man on the moon, but higher than the Vietnam war, Watergate, the United Nations, NATO and the Panama Canal, is the Beatles' first U.S. TV appearance, in 1964.

- A&E Television Network polled over 300 distinguished world leaders and scholars for their *"Biography of the Millennium,* the 100 Most Influential People of the Last 1000 Years. The Beatles, "new leaders of a cultural revolution," ranked 76th, ahead of Stalin, Marconi (inventor of radio,) Oppenheimer ("Father of the atomic bomb,") DaGuerre (inventor of photography,) Ronald Reagan and Suleiman the Magnificent.

- On the 25th anniversary of the Beatles' 1967 *Sergeant Pepper* album, Ted Koppel called it "an epochal event in the history of western civilization."

- In a 2003 TV special Moscow's Red Square was packed with thousands of all ages, including pre-teens, singing the old Beatles' songs with Sir Paul McCartney. Many older people were in tears. It was almost like a religious experience. Between songs Russian historians discussed how the Beatles helped topple communism. *Topple communism? The Beatles! Nah.* Read on:

The Beatles were banned by the USSR, so they became the generation's secret symbol of freedom. Both Presidents Putin and Gorbachev admitted to having been Beatles fans, listening in secret on Luxembourg Radio. Gorbachev said, "The music of the Beatles taught the young people of the Soviet Union that there is another life—there is freedom elsewhere." Putin said, "Their music was a dose of freedom, like an open window to the world."

Russian historian Arteme Troitsky said, "The Beatles have done more toward the fall of the Soviet Union than any other Western institution. They started a whole new movement in the Soviet Union, involving millions of young people." Another Russian historian added, "The Beatles were affecting the superstructure of the society and *it literally brought about that change that caused the collapse of the whole system.*"

Outwardly, the events played out on the international stage of politics and diplomacy, starring Ronald Reagan and Mikhael Gorbachov.

In the heavenlies, great angelic battles were fought and won through the intercessory prayers of the saints.

But behind the scenes on earth, music played an astonishing role.

We now see that the movement the Beatles epitomized has changed the history, not just of western civilization, but of the world. Half a generation ago in much of the world, we would have heard music strange and foreign to our western ears. Each culture, in relative isolation for centuries, had developed its own system of music and cultural distinctives. But today in many cultures what you are bombarded with is the pop music of the western nations, although sometimes with a refreshing local flavor.

Broken Barriers

This worldwide movement of popular music has broken down many of the tribal barriers that once separated nations. It has become a universal language, uniting the young of almost all nations into one great body of music lovers.

The Explosive Potential

Now, here's the point of all this: **If secular music can change the world, can you *imagine* the explosive potential of genuinely Holy Spirit-anointed music to change the world for God?** What does this mean for the Christian musician seeking his or her role in the fulfillment of the Great Commission in the 21st century?

There has never been such a time as this for Christian music. *Newsweek* magazine said in a 2003 cover story, "Contemporary Christian Music is now the hottest" (fastest rising) "genre in the entire music industry …with more than twenty major Christian music festivals a year, some drawing up to 100,000 attendees … for every ten country albums sold, seven Christian CDs fly off the shelf…Sales topped the combined numbers of jazz, classical and New Age." Isn't that interesting? People are listening to Christian music… *Whoa! Rewind!* Did you catch that? Sales topped *the combined numbers of jazz, classical and New Age!*" People *are listening* to Christian music!

But let's take it one step further: **Worship music is now the most vital sector of Contemporary Christian Music.** In one recent week numbers 1, 2 and 3 on Billboard Magazine's CCM chart were live worship albums. After 19 years, two Grammies, 34 Dove awards and an American Music Award in the pop category, Michael W. Smith's first worship album topped all his previous efforts. Many CCM artists are now making worship albums.

Time/Life, who for years have sold music collections through TV ads—favorite artists, hits, rock, jazz, country, all kinds of pop—were amazed when their first Worship collection turned out to be the fastest selling item they had ever had.

Now, on the surface all those numbers may sound crassly commercial, but please understand our motivation in citing them. It isn't to tempt you to try and become rich and famous, but to encourage you—now is your time as a Christian musician! This is your call, your challenge! Do you see what is happening? **The whole pop music phenomenon of the past forty years and more has been a setup for you—a giant sting operation!** The devil may have meant it for his purposes, but God in His higher purposes has allowed it to prepare a generation throughout the world for what is perhaps the final harvest. A.W. Tozer said, **"God's purpose in redemption is to make worshipers out of rebels**." And modern worship music has become a powerful evangelistic tool. People being won to the Lord today through worship music start right out in their new lives as worshipers!

So here we have a modern-day "missionary" phenomenon: In all of these different places, tied together by a common musical culture, **the harvest field is ripe for sold-out musicians. What an opportunity! What a responsibility!**

Let your music change minds and lives and cultures. Learn to write great stuff, full of imagery, hooks, emotion, energy…and God's truth. Then, if you have a mandate from Him, go sing it on the street corners, in the parks, in the churches, the halls, the arenas. Don't wait for some hot agent to get you big money for a "gig;" go where the needs are, whenever you get a chance. We're not saying you shouldn't make a living from your songs and your ministry if God allows; we're saying, don't let that be your goal or your guide.

Go for it!

Remember that your gift is a trust for which you must give account.

But enjoy it.

Revel in it.

Thank God for it.

Worship with it.

Practice long.

Listen a lot.

Jam hard, as hard as an athlete exercises.

Master your music, don't let its seductive power master you.

Do you want to be a star? "They that turn many to righteousness (shall shine) as the stars for ever and ever." (Daniel 12:3). Do you long to be the greatest? Try Jesus' method: be a servant (Mark 10:43,44). If God is calling you, throw yourself into the harvest field where your gift will count for eternity. Get yourself trained and prepared both musically and spiritually, and go for it!

When the earth
gives its final shake;
when our castles and
fortresses
and towers
and monu-
ments have
collapsed,
and when
all the dust
has settled,

THE WORD
OF GOD

will still be
standing
there,
unmoved.
It is Truth
and safety
and eternal life.
So now I will mine
that Word eagerly, as if it
were gold.Then I will write it
down and sing it out, loud and clear,
so the nations can hear it and be saved.

APPLICATION:

Now, here's the final application. The Songwriter's Checklist. We hope you'll use it every time you write a song. **Check your song against this list to discover its potential weaknesses, then improve it before releasing it.** (It will work for any kind of song, not just worship songs.)

CHECKLIST FOR SONGWRITERS (OR SELECTORS)

God Songs, by Paul Baloche and Jimmy and Carol Owens

Qualities Common to Successful Songs:

Specifics

1. **The Very Idea.** Universal and striking and uplifting, worth writing a song about

2. **Emotional Impact.** Create an *experience*. Make us *feel* and *care*. (A built-in cry?)

3. **Hooks.** Lyric, melodic, rhythmic, vocal, instrumental, etc. Placement of hooks

4. **Repetition.** In lyrics, melody, chord progressions, rhythm patterns

5. **Title.** Short and colorful. Paint a picture. Same as the main hook if possible

6. **Style.** Identifiable and authentic: in language, tone, harmony, melody and rhythm.

7. **Timeliness or Timelessness**

8. **Form.** Verse-chorus or AABA, for example. Build something or take us somewhere.

Lyrics

9. **Rhyme.** Perfect or imperfect. Good use of assonance, etc. Consistent patterns

10. **Straight-ahead lyrics.** No backward phrases (except in lofty or scripture songs)

11. **Lyrics easy to sing.** Syllables flow, words roll off the tongue, accents fall in the right places, tones make the voice sound and feel great

12. **Lyrics easy to hear**

13. **Lyrics easy to understand.** No secret code, no explanation required

14. **Strong opening lines.** Set theme or conflict quickly.

15. **Snapshots.** Distilled lyrics—descriptive, sensory phrases, action words

16. **Fresh camera angles.** Distinctive point of view. Avoid cliches.

17. **Focus.** Make one point and develop it.

18. **Grammatical correctness**

19. **Theological correctness**

Music

20. **Interesting melody.** A tune you can "ride on"

21. **Melodic range.** At least an octave (for dramatic effect), not over an 11th (for singability), or small range (for quiet or worshipful atmosphere)

22. **The Right Key.** A worship song must be in the common range (A) B♭ up to D (E♭).

23. **Appropriate harmony.** A worship song needs to be harmonically simple but colorful.

24. **Appropriate rhythm.** To suit the message

25. **Unity in Variety.** Cohesive, but with rhythmic and melodic variation

General

26. **Prosody.** Appropriate "wedding" of words and music. All the elements working together to enhance the feeling of the message (The Cardinal Rule)

27. **Logical progression** of words and music. (A worship song needs to be sequential and predictable, for quick learning.)

28. **Simplicity.** Only one complex element at a time (lyrics, melody, harmony, rhythm)

29. **Uniqueness:** What is *special* about this song, to make it stand out among others?

30. **Spiritual content and anointing.** Hear what the Holy Spirit is saying and let Him say it through you.

All these things together will make your song easy to learn, easy to remember and hard to forget.

Let us make one more suggestion: While all this material is fresh in your memory, take a few minutes to skim through the book again, this time reading just the headings and bolded lines, to implant the concepts in your mind. Happy hunting!

Paul, Jimmy and Carol

APPENDIX 1
SONG TYPES THAT HAVE NOT MADE IT

(Qualities Common to unsuccessful songs. Mark these mistakes and avoid them.)

1. **The Wimpy Idea.** A song about an idea not worth writing a song about.

2. **The Ho Hum Hymn, or Boring Ballad.** No emotional impact. Who cares?

3. **The Mongrel, or Mixed Breed** (Genus Anonymous). It can't make up its mind what *style* it's supposed to be.

4. **The Up-the-Wall Air.** So much repetition it drives the listener crazy

5. **The Empty Fishing Line.** Where's the hook?

6. **The Blob.** No form, or ABCDEFG. Also known as the Rambling Rose or the Wandering Minstrel Show

7. **The Marathon.** Much too long for the listener's attention span

8. **The Cliche Collection.** Filled with trite rhymes and cloying cliches

9. **The Lumbering Lyric.** Words that don't "sing"

10. **The Secret Message.** Written in religious terms only the initiated can understand

11. **The Late Bloomer.** All the good stuff saved until after the audience has tuned out

12. **The Shotgun Blast.** Shoot off a blast of ideas—maybe one will bring down a bird. Also known as the Variety Show

13. **The Two-Way Stretch.** Range is too wide.

14. **The Jumping Jack.** Too much happening at once for the listener to grasp

15. **The Unhappy Marriage.** A "bad wedding" of words and music

16. **The Turf War.** One or more of the elements fighting the message

17. **The Boogaloo Prayer.** "Heavenly Father, we come humbly boogying before Thy throne."

18. **The Sick Joke.** A finger snapping, grooving, grinning song about Jesus dying

19. **The Crossed-up Crossover.** A Christian song caught sneaking about in disguise. We aren't sure whether it's addressed to the Lord or to a lover.

20. **The Doctrinal Dissertation,** or "Everything you've always wanted to know about Christianity, in one song." Also known as the Theological Thesis

21. The Dry Well. A Christian song with no Living Water

22. The Cookie. Shaped by a cookie cutter, with nothing to distinguish it from others in its genre

23. The Copycat. Oops! Too close for comfort! Or Imitation is the sincerest form of plagiarism.

Some songs have only a line or two that fit into these categories and can be easily fixed. A combination of two or more, such as the Lumbering Blob or the Unhappily Married Mongrel, usually indicates a basic lack of understanding of what a song is supposed to be.

APPENDIX 2
THE ABC'S OF MUSIC

The Names of Notes

The easy way to remember the notes of the staff is by means of acronyms. Remember these two words: *Boys* and *Cows*. Starting from the bottom up:

The notes on the lines of the treble clef are **E**very **G**ood **B**oy **D**oes **F**ine.

The notes on the lines of the bass clef are **G**ood **B**oys **D**o **F**ine **A**cts.

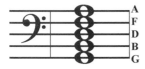

The notes in the spaces of the treble clef are **F**ood **A**ll **C**ows **E**at?

The note is the spaces of the bass clef are **A**ll **C**ows **E**at **G**rass.

Those short lines above and below the staff are called *ledger lines.*

Accidentals

An accidental alters the pitch of a note.

- A *sharp* ♯ raises the pitch by a half tone.

- A *flat* ♭ lowers the pitch by a half tone.

- A *double sharp* ✕ raises the pitch by a whole tone.

- A *double flat* ♭♭ lowers the pitch by a whole tone.

- A *natural* ♮ raises or lowers the pitch of a flatted or sharped note by a half tone or cancels the effect of a previously established accidental.

- An accidental affects all recurrences of the same tone within the same measure. If an altered tone is extended by means of a *tie* beyond a single bar, the pitch remains the same as long as the tie continues.

Intervals

The term *interval* is simply a way of describing how many scale tones there are between one note and the next in a melody or a chord.

- The same note repeated is called a *prime* interval.

- The next note up or down the scale is called a 2nd, or *step* interval.

- Any interval wider than a 2nd is called a *leap* interval.
  Learn to identify intervals by the way they look on the staff. Instead of counting the steps from one tone to another, remember this: *odd numbers are even, and even numbers are odd.* Look at these intervals and you'll see what we mean:

Example 1

Notice that in intervals having odd numbers, 3, 5, 7, 9, etc., both notes are even, that is, both are on either lines or spaces. A 5th, for example G up to D (or D down to G—it's the same interval either way) has both tones on lines, two lines apart. A 5th (F up to C) has both tones on spaces, two spaces apart. Likewise a 7th will be three lines or three spaces apart, etc.

Intervals having even numbers, 2, 4, 6, octave, etc., are the reverse—they are on odd lines and spaces. A 6th (D up to B) is two spaces plus one line up.

This doesn't mean these intervals are all the same number of half steps apart, simply that they are that many *scale* steps apart. An interval on two adjacent lines will always be some kind of a 3rd, but the key signature or an accidental or the tones' relative positions in the scale will determine whether it's a major or minor 3rd.

For example, in the key of E major, which has four sharps (F,C,G and D), the E on the bottom of the treble staff is natural and is the tonic, or starting note, of the scale. The note on the line above it is a G#, the 3rd of the scale, so the interval is a *major* 3rd. However, in the key of C, where there are no sharps or flats, those same lines contain an E natural and a G *natural*, the 3rd and 5th of the C major scale, so the interval is a *minor* 3rd.

Practice singing these scale intervals with an instrument until you can do it easily in your mind just by looking at the written music. Don't worry about the sharp and flat keys until you've mastered the scale intervals in the key of C. Once you understand how to determine what key you're in, the principle is a shortcut for sightsinging in all keys.

Numerals

There are two kinds of numerals used in music notation:

- **Roman numerals** (I, ii, iii, etc.) denote the position of chords within a scale. Two Roman numerals with a slant between them, for example IV/V, (pronounced "four over five,") indicate a chord built on the IVth interval of the scale over a bass note which is the Vth of the scale, as in F/G in the key of C major. The unaltered I, IV and V chords are all major, and the ii, iii, vi are minor. The vii is diminished.

- **Arabic numerals** (1, 2, 3, etc, or 2nd, 3rd, 4th, etc) indicate:

    a. the position of notes within a chord

    b. the number of steps between consecutive notes in a melody or in a chord, including both notes.

Scales, Triads and 7th Chords

Let's look first at a major scale. C major is the easiest of all to visualize because it contains no sharps or flats.

Example 2

Note that all the tones are two half steps (one whole step) apart except the interval from 3 to 4, and from 7 to octave, which are one half step apart.

- The octave, 4th and 5th intervals are called *perfect* intervals. When lowered a half step the 4th and 5th are called *diminished* intervals.

- The 2nd, 3rd, 6th and 7th are called *major* intervals. When lowered a half step they are called *minor* intervals. (Note: In common usage, the lowered 7th, while technically a minor 7th, is usually referred to simply as a 7th.)

- Perfect and major intervals, when extended a half step, are called *augmented* intervals.

Now, let's build simple three-note chords (called *triads*) on top of the scale tones.

Example 3

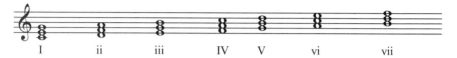

I ii iii IV V vi vii

- In a major scale, the unaltered I, IV and V chords are *major chords*. This means it takes two whole steps to span from the root of the chord to the 3rd, which is the next tone up in the triad.

- The ii, iii and vi chords in a major scale are *minor chords*, each having one and a half steps between the root and the 3rd.

- The vii chord in a major scale is a *diminished chord*, which means that in addition to the one and a half steps from the root to the third, there are also one and a half steps from the 3rd to the 5th.

Now let's add one more notch to each triad.

Example 4

IMaj7 iim7 iiim7 IVMaj7 V7 vim7 viim7(b5)

They now become various kinds of *7th chords*, or *tetrads*. The unaltered V7, built on the 5th degree of the scale, is called a *dominant 7th chord*.

And to add to the richness, they can be *extended*, to 9ths, 11ths and 13ths, by stacking notes in 3rds on top of them.

(Actually, the 13th in modern harmony nomenclature is a slightly different animal—it's merely a dominant 7th chord with an added 13th.)

And chords can be *altered*, by raising or lowering the pitch of one or more of the tones by means of *accidentals:* sharps, flats or naturals placed in front of the tones.

Chords can be *voiced* in either open or close position. Extended and altered chords are usually found in open position, which allows some "breathing room" between the tones.

So far we've mentioned only *major scales.* There are also several types of *minor scales.* Minor scales have the 3rd lowered a half step, which is what distinguishes them as minor scales. But some of them also contain alterations of other tones.

Example 5: (Minor Scales)
Pure Minor (Natural Minor)

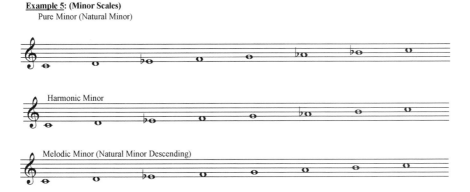

And these scales, with their chords, can begin on any one of the twelve chromatic tones.

Example 6

In addition there are other types of scales available to us, such as pentatonic (five-tone) scales, blues scales, whole tone scales, modes and various ethnic scales, all of which make modern harmony very rich indeed. But all that is material for a whole book. Again let us recommend "Writing Music for Hit Songs," by Jai Josefs (Schirmer Books).

Key Signatures

The *key signature* identifies what key the song is in.

C major has no sharps or flats.

F major has one flat. After that, a flat major key is called by the next to last flat in its key signature.

A *relative minor key* shares the same key signature as its major counterpart, but starts a minor 3rd below the major key.

A major key in sharps is called by the tone one half step above the last sharp in the key signature. For instance, in one sharp the sharp is on the F line; therefore the key is G major. In two sharps the key is D major, a half step up from the C#.

Symbols Within Chord Symbols

There are a few other symbols used to identify chords. (We'll use C for convenience:)

- An augmented chord (a major triad with a raised, or augmented 5th) is designated C aug, or more commonly C+

- A diminished chord (a minor triad with a lowered, or diminished 5th) is indicated in one of these two ways:

- A diminished 7th chord is a diminished chord with a *doubly* diminished 7th added, which makes the 7th enharmonic with, or the same tone as, a 6th. It is designated C dim7 or C°7

This chord is perfectly symmetrical, its four tones equidistant in any inversion.

- A half-diminished 7th is

However, in pop music this chord is usually called by another name, Cm7b5, which spells out the notes contained in it.

- There's also a kind of studio shorthand which calls a #9 a +9 or a b9 a -9, for instance, but in this book we'll stick with the #'s and b's to avoid confusion.

Tempo

Tempo is the speed of the music. There is a set of Italian words used in classical music to indicate tempo, but in pop music English words are usually used, such as slowly, moderately, fast, etc. In this techno-pop generation, *metronome markings* are very important. Tempo is measured by a metronome in beats per minute.

for example, ♩ = *128*.

The Italian words are still used pretty much for tempo changes. *Accellerando* (Accell.) means speed up gradually, *Ritard* (Rit.) and *Rallentando* (Rall.) both mean slow down, but Rall. usually happens near the end of a piece and is used for a more marked slowing down. *A tempo* (pronounced *ah tempo*) means return to the original tempo.

Note Values

The duration of a note is indicated in writing by its shape. These are the note values in Common Time:

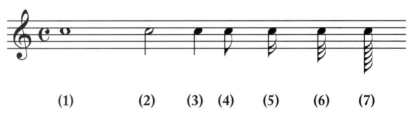

(1)   (2)   (3) (4)   (5)   (6)   (7)

(1) Whole note = 4 beats

(2) Half note = 2 beats

(3) Quarter note = 1 beat

(4) Eighth note = 1/2 beat

(5) Sixteenth note = 1/4 beat

(6) Thirty-second note = 1/8 beat

(7) Sixty-fourth note = 1/16 beat

Notes shorter than quarter notes, when in sequence, use *beams* rather than flags on their stems to group them together.

A dot added after a note increases its value by one half.

(The British system has different names for them. They are, in the same order: Semibreve, minim, crotchet, Quaver, Semiquaver, Demisemiquaver, Hemidemisemiquaver.)

Rests: A rest is a moment of silence. Rests have the same time values as their equivalent notes and are notated thus:

Rests: Whole   1/2   1/4   1/8   1/16   1/32   1/64

Triplets: three notes in the space normally occupied by two. The notes are bracketed together and marked with a 3. Or it may work the other way around, as in two eighth notes against a beat in 6/8 time for example.

Time Signatures

The lower half tells us what kind of note gets a beat. The upper tells us how many beats there are in a measure.

4/4 means there are four quarter notes in a measure.

C (*Common time)* means exactly the same as 4/4.

C with a slash through it stands for *Cut time,* meaning the time is cut in half; therefore it takes two quarter notes or a half note to equal one beat. Cut time feels just like 2/4. (Also called *alla breve.)*

6/8 means an eighth note gets a beat and there are six eighths in a bar.

At moderate to faster tempos it becomes awkward to conduct every half beat, so we beat 2/4 and 6/8 each with two beats to the bar, 9/8 with three beats to the bar and 12/8 with four.

Volume

Volume is a measure of the loudness of the music. The Italian abbreviations are used consistently in pop music.

pp   (*pianissimo*)=very soft

p   (*piano*)=soft

mp   (*mezzopiano*)=moderately soft

mf   (*mezzoforte*)=moderately loud

f   (*forte*)=loud

ff   (*fortissimo*)=very loud

Dynamics

Dynamics markings indicate an increase or decrease in volume. *Crescendo (Cresc.)* means get louder gradually. It's marked:

Diminuendo (Dim.) means get gradually softer. It's marked:

Other Markings

(1)　(2)　　(3)　　(4) (5)(6)　(7)　　　　　(8)　　　(9)　　　　　　　(10)

(1) A bar line separates measures, or bars.

(2) A double bar line separates sections of music.

(3) An *Accent* mark means attack the note hard.

(4) *Sforzando* means attack the note hard, instantly reduce volume to soft, then crescendo back to loud during the duration of the note.

(5) A dot over a note (*staccato*) means play or sing the note short.

(6) A line over a note means broaden the note.

(7) A *tie* links two notes on the same pitch together to lengthen the note value.

(8) A *slur* ties together two or more notes that are to be articulated smoothly, without separate attacks.

(9) A long curving line over a series of notes is a *phrase mark*, meaning perform the whole phrase smoothly, in one breath (*legato.*)

(10) A *fermata* , also called a *pause* or *hold,* indicates the tempo is momentarily suspended and the note is to be held longer than its normal duration.

Following the Roadmap

Several signs guide the musician around a chart. Rather than recopy sections that are repeated exactly, we use repeat signs to direct us back to the

beginning of a section to be repeated. Often the material doesn't end the same way both times, so we use 1st and 2nd endings (or even 3rd endings.)

Sometimes we want to jump back over two or more sections and repeat material, so we use either *D.S. al fine* (pronounced "fee-nay") or *D.S. al Coda*.

D.S. al fine means go back to the 𝄋 sign and play from there to a point marked *fine* and end there.

D.S. al Coda means go back to the sign 𝄋 and play to the ⊕ marker, then jump to the ⊕ *Coda* , which is a section at the very end of the chart.

If we want to go all the back to the beginning, we use *D.C. (da capo)* instead of *D.S. (dal segno).*

GLOSSARY

A CAPPELLA: unaccompanied

ALLITERATION: beginning two or more syllables of a word group with the same sound: Heavenly host

ANAPHORA: repetition of a word or words at the beginning of two or more verses or lines

ASSONANCE: agreement of vowel sounds; rhyme in which the same vowels are used with different consonants, as in time/line

BOOKENDS: a hook lyric line, often the title, placed both at the beginning and the end of a song or chorus

BRIDGE: a section of a song that "bridges" from one section to the next

BUILT-IN CRY: a line of longing or triumph or passion, accompanied by the highest, most emotional music in a song

CACOPHONY: (in lyrics) a series of syllables with harsh sounding effect ("crash bang lyrics"); (in music) harsh, crashing, bashing, discordant sounds

CHANNEL: a short musical passage leading from one section of a song to another

CHORUS: the section containing the main theme and hook line of a song, usually repeated with both words and music the same each time

CLIMB: a short musical channel with a climbing profile that links two passages of a song

CLUSTERING: in lyric writing, a method of organizing ideas, in which all the related thoughts are gathered together prior to organizing and sequencing them.

COMMON RANGE: the vocal range of the average person, generally low Bb up to D, with occasional brief stretches at either end

CONSONANCE: similarity of consonants or groups of consonants, especially at the ends of words, as in strong and ring.

CONVERSATIONAL SINGING: using syncopation to place accents where they would occur in speech

COUNTERMELODY: a secondary melody sounded at the same time as the main melody

CRASH BANG LYRICS: our coinage for the use of successive hard consonants and harsh vowel sounds in lyrics to achieve a crashing, banging effect (cacophony)

CRESCENDO: a gradual increase in loudness

DISSONANCE: a simultaneous combination of musical tones creating a feeling of unrest and needing resolution

DOMINANT: the 5th step of the scale, or a chord based on that tone

DYNAMICS: variation in volume, intensity and expression

ELEMENTS (of a song): Intangible elements—Message, style, atmosphere, mood

Tangible elements—Form, lyrics, melody, harmony, rhythm

EUPHONY: the flowing together of pleasant sounds (Contrast cacophony)

EXPANDED RHYME: second word of the couplet has added letters: pray/ways; believe/received (Contrast reduced rhyme)

FIGURE: a recurring musical line or pattern, usually in an accompaniment

FEEL (See under Rhythm)

FILL: an improvised instrumental figure, usually bridging between the end of a line and the beginning of the next

GENRE: a fancy word for style

GROOVE (See under Rhythm)

HOOK: a device in a song that grabs and holds the attention of the listener

Main hook: the combination of the principal point of the message with the most prominent musical passage of the song, repeated often

Secondary hook: a repeated instrumental figure, production effect or vocal sound, or possibly a structural device such as anaphora

INNER RHYME: rhyme occurring within the same line

INTERLUDE: an instrumental section inserted between vocal sections

INTERVAL: the number of steps encompassed by two consecutive tones, either horizontally, in melody, or vertically, in harmony

INVERSION: a chord with any note other than the root on the bottom

LEAP INTERVAL: any melodic interval larger than a whole step (See Step interval)

LICK: an improvised embellishment

METAPHOR: a word or phrase that implies comparison with another object or concept, as in "You are a rose." (Compare simile)

MODULATION: changing from one key to another

MOTIF: (or motive) a recurring musical theme

NEAR RHYME: rhyme that depends on similarity of sounds, as in time/shine, as distinct from perfect rhyme, as in play/say

PARALELLISM: The deliberate repetition of particular words or sentence structures for effect, as in "You rule, You reign"

PERSONIFICATION: the humanization of an object or animal, endowing it with human attributes, such as speaking or feeling

PASSING TONE: a non-chordal tone that moves stepwise between two chord tones.

PROSODY: in poetry, the study of poetic meters and versification; in songwriting, the wedding of words and music

REDUCED RHYME: first word of the couplet has added letters: sings/bring; cares/share (Contrast expanded rhyme)

REFRAIN: a line or couplet repeated at the end of each stanza or chorus

RELATIVE MINOR: the minor key with the same key signature as a given major key. The minor key begins two scale notes below the major key.

RHYME SCHEME: the pattern of rhymes used in a lyric or poem

RHYTHM: consisting of several components:

Tempo, or speed

Rhythm pattern—a designation of how many beats per bar, whether straight eighths or dotted eighths and sixteenths, any recurrent syncopation, etc.

Groove—the way the rhythm pattern is played, whether loose and laid-back, or tight and driving; buoyant and on the beat, or spongy and unsettled

Feel— rhythmic buoyancy, created by subtle dynamic gradations and nuances in playing or singing

RHYTHM PATTERN (See under Rhythm)

ROOT: the foundational note on which a chord is built (not to be confused with tonic, the first note of a scale) A root may or may not be the bottom note of a particular voicing.

SEQUENTIAL WRITING: melody writing which leads logically in a predictable manner from one line to the next according to a pattern established in the first two lines of a section

SIMILE: a figure of speech using "like" or "as," in which two things are explicitly compared, as in "You are like a rose," or "You are as beautiful as a rose." (Compare metaphor)

SLANT RHYME: a form of near rhyme in which the same opening and closing consonants are used, as in sail/soul; love/leave

STEP INTERVAL: a melodic interval of a step or half step (See Leap interval)

STANDARD: a song that has endured in popularity for years

SYNCOPATION: a shifting of the normal musical accent, usually by stressing the unaccented beats

TAG ENDING: the ending of a song in which the last line or phrase is repeated one or more times

TEMPO (See under Rhythm)

TESSITURA: the general range of pitch of a voice or instrument in an arrangement

TONIC: the starting note of the scale of the key in which a song is written

TRUE RHYME: perfect rhyme, as in love/above

VERSE: that part of a song following the introduction and preceding the chorus

VOICE LEADING: the way notes resolve within chord changes

VOICING: the way the notes of a chord are arranged, either in open or close harmony

WRAP-AROUND LINE: a line of verse that carries a thought over into the next line (also called a run-on line)

ABOUT THE AUTHORS

Paul Baloche

One of the most prominent praise and worship songwriters of our generation describes his writing as "journaling the process of my walk with the Lord".

Award winning songwriter, Paul Baloche, has authored over 120 recorded songs that have been featured on a variety of albums including the platinum selling WoW Worship CDs and the Time Life - Songs 4 Worship series.

You have probably sung Paul's songs in church or heard his music on albums from well known artists such as Michael W. Smith, Sonicflood, John Tesh, Ron Kenoly, or Don Moen. He has written many popular songs including, "Open the Eyes of My Heart," "Above All," "I Love to be in Your Presence," and "Revival Fire Fall."

An accomplished songwriter, worship leader, and producer for Integrity Music, His own album credits include He Is Faithful, First Love, Open The Eyes Of My Heart, and his most recent project, God of Wonders. In addition to these recordings, he has produced four albums for Maranatha! Music's Praise Band.

As a worship leader, Paul's unpretentious and approachable style has encouraged many to draw near to God in worship. "I want my music, and more importantly my life," Paul explains, "to inspire people to pursue a sincere, authentic relationship with Christ."

Through God's leading, he was introduced to Dan and Kelly Willard, and later to Lenny LeBlanc. As a guitarist and vocalist, he accompanied them on worship oriented concert tours. "Their lives taught me so much about humility, honesty, and presenting a sincere faith," says Paul.

A longtime member and producer of the Maranatha! Praise Band, Paul has traveled the world teaching and leading others in worship. He has performed in South Africa, Europe, Singapore, Australia and New Zealand, where many of his songs have become favorite choruses sung by people of all denominations.

In addition to his songwriting success, Paul has been playing guitar and teaching professionally for over 20 years. He is a graduate of The Grove School of Music in Studio City, California and has developed a series of 90-minute videos that are designed to help musicians expand their guitar-playing skills, equipping them to play some of the more challenging praise and worship styles of today.

For twelve years he has served as the Worship Pastor at Community Christian Fellowship Church in Lindale, Texas, where he lives with his wife Rita and their three children.

Jimmy and Carol Owens

Jimmy and Carol are among the pioneers of Contemporary Christian Music and the modern worship movement. They are composers of some 250 published and recorded songs, including 12 musicals. They have taught songwriting for over twenty-five years. As founders of *School of Music Ministries International,* Jimmy and Carol, with their teams of artist/teachers, have strengthened both the technical skills and spiritual foundations of thousands of musicians, worship leaders and songwriters around the world.

Before specializing with Carol in songwriting and teaching, Jimmy was a church minister of music and an arranger/conductor for two TV series and many albums on most major Christian labels.

Their award-winning *Come Together* was the first of the large arena Praise and Worship musicals. It, and their prayer musical, *If My People,* have been widely embraced by the church in many nations. Their *Heal Our Land* has been performed in many city-wide events.

The Owens's dramatic musicals, such as *Show Me!*, *The Glory of Christmas* and *The Witness* have brought thousands to faith in Christ, and their children's musicals (*Ants'hillvania* and others) have taught God's ways to multitudes of enthusiastic kids. Their worship songs, such as "Freely, Freely" and "Holy, Holy" are in many modern hymnals and are used worldwide.

Jimmy and Carol live in Southern California, near the families of their children. Jamie Owens Collins is a recording artist, songwriter and speaker. Her husband, Dan Collins, is a record producer and publisher. Buddy Owens serves with Pastor Rick Warren on the pastoral staff of Saddleback Community Church and as Editorial Director for Purpose Driven Ministries.

SONG COPYRIGHT INFORMATION

Other Songs/Composers Mentioned

All Hail the Power of Jesus' Name	Edward Perronet, Adapted by John Rippon
Amazing Grace	John Newton/Traditional American melody
Ancient of Days	Jamie Harvill/Gary Sadler
As the Deer	Marty Nystrom
Better is One Day	Matt Redman
Breathe	Marie Barnett
Change My Heart, O God	Eddie Espinosa
Christ the Lord is Risen Today	Charles Wesley
Come Thou Fount of Every Blessing	Robert Robinson, Adapted by Margaret Clarkson
Crown Him with Many Crowns	Matthew Bridges/George J. Elvey
Emmanuel	Bob McGee
Every Move I Make	David Ruis
Fairest Lord Jesus	Anonymous German hymn/Schlesische Volkslieder
For All the Saints	William H. How/Ralph Vaughan Williams
Give Thanks	Henry Smith
God of Wonders	Marc Byrd/Steve Hindalong
Great is the Lord	Michael W. And Deborah Smith
Great is Thy Faithfulness	Thomas O.Chisom/William M. Runyan
Hallelujah (Your Love is Amazing)	Brenton Brown and Brian Doerksen
He is Exalted	Twila Paris
Heaven is in My Heart	Graham Kendrick
Holy, Holy, Holy	Reginald Heber/John B. Dykes
Hosanna	Carl Tuttle
Humble King	Brenton Brown
I Could Sing of Your Love Forever	Martin Smith

I Love You Lord	Laurie Klein
I Will Not Forget You	Ben and Robin Pasley
I Worship You, Almighty God	Sondra Corbett Wood
In the Secret	Andy Park
Isn't He?	John Wimber
It Came Upon a Midnight Clear	Edmund H. Sears/Richard H. Willis
Jesus, Name Above All Names	Naida Hearn
Joy to the World	Isaac Watts/George Frederick Handel
Let Everything that Has Breath	Matt Redman
Let it Rise	Holland Davis
Let the River Flow	Darrell Evans
Light the Fire Again	Brian Doerksen
Lord, I Give You My Heart	Reuben Morgan
Lord Reign in Me	Brenton Brown
More Love, More Power	Jude Del Hierro
My Jesus, I Love Thee	William R. Featherston/Adoniram J. Gordon
My Life is in You, Lord	Daniel Gardner
O Worship the King	Robert Grant/William Gardiner's Sacred Melodies
Over the Rainbow	E.Y. Harburg/Harold Arlen
The Potter's Hand	Darlene Zschech
Praise the Name of Jesus	Roy Hicks, Jr.
Praise to the Lord, the Almighty	Joachim Neander, tr. By Catherine Winkworth/anon
Rise Up and Praise Him	Paul Baloche/Gary Sadler
The River is Here	Andy Park
Shout to the North	Martin Smith
Silent Night	Joseph Mohr, tr. by John F. Young/Franz Gruber
Something About That Name	Bill and Gloria Gaither
Step By Step	Rich Mullins
The Church's One Foundation	Samuel J. Stone/Samuel S. Wesley
The King of Love My Shepherd Is	Henry W. Baker/John B. Dykes
There is a Fountain	William Cowper/Traditional American melody
There is None Like You	Lennie LeBlanc
To Him Who Sits on the Throne	D. Graafsma
Trading My Sorrows	Darrell Evans
Victory Chant	Joseph Vogels
When I Survey the Wondrous Cross	Isaac Watts/based on a Gregorian chant
When You Wish Upon a Star	Ned Washington/Leigh Harline
You Are My Hiding Place	Michael Ledner

SCRIPTURES RELATING TO WORSHIP

1 CHRONICLES 15 (NKJV)

*28. Thus all Israel brought up the ark of the
covenant of the LORD with shouting,
and with the sound of the horn, with trumpets, and with cymbals,
making music with stringed instruments and harps.*

1 CHRONICLES 16 (NKJV)

*7. And on that day David first delivered
this psalm into the hand of
Asaph and his brethren, to thank the LORD.
8. Oh, give thanks to the LORD!
Call upon his name;
Make known his deeds among the peoples!
9. Sing to Him, sing psalms to Him;
Talk of all His wondrous works!
10. Glory in His holy name;
Let the hearts of those rejoice who seek the LORD!
11. Seek the LORD and His strength;*

Seek His face evermore!
12. Remember His marvelous works which He has done,
His wonders, and the judgments of His mouth....

23. Sing to the LORD, all the earth;
Proclaim the good news of His salvation from day to day.
24. Declare His glory among the nations;
His wonders among all peoples.
25. For the LORD is great and greatly to be praised:
He is also to be feared above all gods.
26. For all the gods of the people are idols,
But the LORD made the heavens.
27. Honor and majesty are before Him;
Strength and gladness are in his place.
28. Give to the LORD, O kindreds of the peoples,
Give to the LORD glory and strength.
29. Give to the LORD the glory due His name:
Bring an offering, and come before Him.
Oh, worship the LORD in the beauty of holiness!
30. Tremble before Him, all the earth.
The world also is firmly established,
It shall not be moved.
31. Let the heavens rejoice, and let the earth be glad,
And let them say among the nations,
"The LORD reigns!"
32. Let the sea roar, and all its fullness;
Let the field rejoice, and all that is in it.
33. Then the trees of the woods shall rejoice before the LORD,
For He is coming to judge the earth.
34. Oh, give thanks to the LORD, for he is good!
For his mercy endures forever...

36b. And all the people said, "Amen!" and praised the LORD.

PSALM 22 (NEW LIVING TRANSLATION)

27. The whole earth will acknowledge the
LORD and return to Him.
People from every nation will bow down before Him.
28. For the LORD is king! He rules over all the nations.

PSA 33:3 (NKJV)

Sing to Him a new song; play skilfully with a shout of joy.

PSA 47:1 (NKJV)

O clap your hands, all you peoples! Shout to
God with the voice of triumph!

PSA 85:6,7 (NIV)

Will You not revive us again, that
Your people may rejoice in You?
Show us Your unfailing love, O
LORD, and grant us Your salvation.

PSALM 95 (NKJV)

1. Oh come, let us sing to the LORD!
Let us shout joyfully to the Rock of our salvation.
2. Let us come before His presence with thanksgiving;
Let us shout joyfully to Him with psalms.
3. For the LORD is the great God,
And the great King above all gods...

6. Oh come, let us worship and bow down:
Let us kneel before the LORD our maker.
7. For He is our God,
And we are the people of His pasture,
And the sheep of His hand.

PSALM 98 (NKJV)

4. Shout joyfully to the Lord, all the earth;
Break forth in song, rejoice, and sing praises.
5. Sing to the Lord with the harp,
With the harp and the sound of a psalm,
6. With trumpets and the sound of a horn;
Shout joyfully before the Lord, the King.

PSALM 104:33

I will sing to the Lord as long as I live;
I will sing praise to my God while I have my being.

PSALM 105:2

Sing to Him, sing psalms to Him;
Talk of all His wondrous works.

PSALM 111:1 (NKJV)

Praise the LORD! I will praise the LORD
with my whole heart, in the
assembly of the upright and in the congregation.

Psalm 149:1 (NKJV)

Praise the Lord! Sing to the LORD a new song,
and His praise in the congregation of saints.

Psalm 150

1. Praise the Lord!
Praise God in His sanctuary;
Praise Him in His mighty firmament!
2. Praise Him for His mighty acts;
Praise Him according to His excellent greatness!
3. Praise Him with the sound of the trumpet;
Praise Him with the lute and harp!
4. Praise Him with the timbrel and dance;
Praise Him with stringed instruments and flutes!
5. Praise Him with loud cymbals;
Praise Him with high sounding cymbals!
6. Let everything that has breath praise the Lord.
Praise the Lord!

Isaiah 6 (NKJV)

1b. I saw the LORD sitting on a throne, high and lifted up,
and the train of His robe filled the temple.
2. Above it stood seraphim…
3. And one cried to another and said,
"Holy, holy, holy is the LORD of hosts;
The whole earth is full of His glory!"

I Corinthians 14:15 (NKJV)

. . .I will pray with the spirit,
And I will also pray with the understanding.
I will sing with the spirit,
And I will also sing with the understanding.

Ephesians 5:19 (NKJV)

Speaking to one another in psalms and hymns and spiritual songs,
Singing and making melody in your heart to the Lord.

NOTES

NOTES

Index

Action Words 92
Alliteration 76, 84, 163-164
Altrogge, Mark 189
Anaphora 84
Anderson, Jared 64
Anointing - How to Receive It 209
Appropriateness 160
Arranging & Performance
  Cardinal Rule 160
  Endings 144
  Figures 143
  Fills 144
  Intros 143
  "Licks" - Improvised 142
Assignment, Writing on 34
Assonance 76, 163
Atmosphere 47
Baloche, Rita 31, 35
Bookends 49
Built-in cry 62, 156
Cacophony 74
Call and Response 225
Camera Angles 90
Cardinal Rule 43, 46, 75, 101, 115, 124, 142, 157,
  159, 160
CCLI 43, 61-64, 203
Chimes 75
Cloninger, Claire 177. 178
Clustering 33
Collins, Jamie Owens 92, 293
Consonance 76
Conflict 40-43
Conversational lyrics 76, 80
Co-writing 40, 175-179
Craft, Building 99, 105, 175, 180
Demos 198
Distilled lyrics 94
Doerksen, Brian 37
Dunnagan, Craig 191, 203
Elements of a Song 44, 46
Euphony 74
Fitts, Bob 157
Focus 91
Form 47, 52-58, 92
Founds, Rick 31
Green, Keith 218
Greenhouse Principle 38-40, 53, 99, 180
Harmony 47-63, 113, 120-122, 130-131
Hayford, Jack 209
Hughes, Tim 36

Hymns or Choruses? 215
Imagery 90, 159
Intervals, influence of 101
Kauflin, Bob 216
Kerr, Ed 34, 163, 176, 177
Kraeuter, Tom 198
Larger than Life Words 82-84
LeBlanc, Lennie 39
Lining 224
Lyrics - Organizing 32
Lyrics - Progression of 92
Melisma 74
Melody - An Experience 96
Melodic Development 105
Melodies - How to Find Them 99
Message 44, 46
Metaphors 87
Millard, Bart 28
Mood 47
Motifs 106
Opening lines 88
Origins of Contemporary Christian Music 228
Parallelism 84
Owens, Buddy 211
Personification 84
Phrasing - Backward 80
Poetic Effect 69
Predictability 65
Prosody - Matching Words to Melodies 94-96
Publishing 199
Range 109
Redman, Matt 32, 45, 66, 70, 188, 215
Repetition 63
Rhyme - Head 76
Rhyme - Imperfect 75
Rhyme - Inner 76
Rhyme patterns 79
Rhyme - Perfect 75
Rhyme - Slant 76
Rhymes and Chimes 75
Rhythm 138
  Feel 141
  Groove 140
  Rhythm Patterns 140
  Tempo 140
Right words, The 89
Scale tones, influence of 101
Scripture Songs, Writing 161
Selecting Songs 212
Sensory Images 82, 86
Sequential Writing 65, 106
Similies 87
Simplicity 63

Snapshots 90
Style 150-151
Syncopation 146
Three Ministries 207
Titles 46
Tomlin, Chris 36, 67, 185
Translating 165
Unity in Variety 56, 148
Variety - Rhythmic and Dynamic 148
Visionaries: Handling New Trends 234
Word Flow 81
Word Sounds   70
Worship Evangelism 209, 242
Worship Music: A Worldwide Phenomenon 244
Worship Music - Scriptural Roots 226
Worship Songs, Special Qualities 183
Wrap-Around Lines 98
Writer's Block, Solutions 166
Writer's Tools 172
Zschech, Darlene 19, 26, 30